100 EASY STEAM ACTIVITIES

ACTIVITIES

Awesome Hands-On Projects
for Aspiring Artists and Engineers

ANDREA SCALZO YI

creator of Raising Dragons

PAGE STREET
PUBLISHING CO.

First published in 2019 by
Page Street Publishing Co.
27 Congress Street, Suite 105
Salem, MA 01970
www.pagestreetpublishing.com

Distributed by Macmillan, sales in Canada by The Canadian Manda Group.

23 22 21 20 19   1 2 3 4 5

ISBN-13: 978-1-62414-892-7
ISBN-10: 1-62414-892-1

Library of Congress Control Number: 2019939663

Cover and book design by Meg Baskis for Page Street Publishing Co.
Photography by Chloe LaFrance Photography
Photography on pages 3, 4, 64, 66 and 69 by Andrea Scalzo Yi
Cover and interior illustrations by Sashatigar/Shutterstock.com

Printed and bound in China

DEDICATION

For Tony and our four little dragons—Nate,
Dylan, Oliver & Alexander

CONTENTS

INTRODUCTION

"Mom, I'm bored! What can we do?"

Does this sound familiar? Well, it did in my house, which inspired me to start doing simple STEAM activities with my kids. We ended up having so much fun that I created Raising Dragons (raisingdragons.com) to share our activities with others. I realized quickly, from the overwhelming response to our videos, that millions of other people were looking for simple ideas to engage their kids too. So in addition to Raising Dragons online, I wrote this book to provide you with super simple activities that are easy (using items found around the house), safe (no box cutters or glue guns) and take only a few minutes to set up.

What is STEM/STEAM and why is it important? STEM incorporates elements of Science, Technology, Engineering and Math into activities instead of focusing on each subject separately. STEM activities can spark curiosity and encourage you to experiment, ask questions, make predictions and have fun—all while learning about concepts like chemistry, motion and force. In addition to teaching important life skills such as critical thinking and problem-solving, STEM activities can help you develop a love of learning and an innate curiosity about how the world around you works. STEM activities also give kids a glimpse into the wonderful opportunities and real-world applications for STEM that lie ahead.

STEAM adds art into the mix, which I feel is the most important part of the equation. It's not only imperative for you to learn to build and problem solve, but to do so with a creative and design-focused mentality. What fun is learning about the changing seasons if you can't take a moment to reflect on the beauty of the trees or the seasonal colors of the changing leaves?

From lava lamps (page 20) and dancing grapes (page 29) to mini-catapults (page 58) and marshmallow igloos (page 162), I hope this book becomes your go-to resource when you need a quick idea or fun activity.

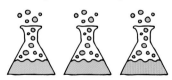

1

SIMPLE SCIENCE EXPERIMENTS

Bringing science into your home with fun, easy experiments is a great way to spark curiosity, learn simple scientific concepts and spend quality time with your siblings and parents, all while engaging in educational activities! The experiments that follow are all SUPER simple to set up and most of them can be done with objects you already have at home. Are you ready? Let's go!

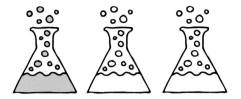

SHAVING CREAM RAIN CLOUDS

This fun, simple science experiment teaches you about weather concepts, and it's lots of fun mixing colors and watching them fall through the shaving cream and into the water. You will want to do this experiment over and over. It never gets old!

MATERIALS

- 1 clear vase or glass jar
- Water
- Shaving cream
- Liquid food coloring
- Droppers

DIRECTIONS

Fill the clear vase about three-quarters full with water. Fill the rest of the vase with shaving cream. Add a few drops each of different colors of food coloring on top of the shaving cream. You will start to see the colors weave their way through the shaving cream cloud and into the water.

If you find it's taking a while for the color to make its way through the cloud, it's probably because you made a very large cloud! In this case, to speed up the process, add some plain water to the clouds to make them heavier and more likely to start falling into the water. Soon you will see lots of beautiful streaks of color making their way into the water.

THE HOWS AND WHYS

As the water gets too heavy for the "cloud," it begins to release it into the "atmosphere" (aka the water), therefore creating "rain."

VARIATIONS

Try making a small cloud and a large cloud. How much longer does it take the coloring to move through the large cloud versus the small cloud? Try making clouds of different colors and mixing various colors like blue and yellow to make the cloud rain green.

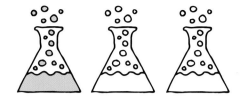

SALTY WATER EGG FLOAT

This simple science experiment demonstrates density and how changing the density of water can make an egg float.

MATERIALS

- 2 clear drinking glasses
- 2 cups (480 ml) water, divided
- 2 raw eggs, divided
- 3 tbsp (54 g) salt

DIRECTIONS

Fill 1 glass with about 1 cup (240 ml) of water. Carefully add 1 egg to the glass and notice how it sinks to the bottom. Add the salt to the second glass and mix in the remaining water. Once the salt is mixed in, add the second egg to the second glass. You will notice the egg in the second glass floats!

THE HOWS AND WHYS

The density of a raw egg is just slightly greater than water, so when it is placed in a cup of water, it will sink to the bottom. If the water is made heavier (or denser) by adding salt, the egg will float when placed in the salty water since it is now lighter than the water.

VARIATION

See if you can adjust the salt level to make the egg float right in the middle of the glass.

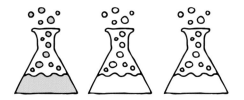

WATER CYCLE IN A BOTTLE

Here's an excellent activity to demonstrate the way water moves through a cycle from liquid to vapor (evaporation) and back to liquid again (condensation), similar to the process of water evaporating into the sky to make clouds and ultimately falling back to earth (precipitation).

MATERIALS

- ½ cup (120 ml) water
- 1 clear plastic water bottle
- Liquid food coloring (optional)
- Black marker

DIRECTIONS

Pour the water into the bottle and add a few drops of food coloring (if using). Seal the bottle and place it in an area with lots of sunlight. Draw some waves, clouds and a sun on the bottle with the black marker. Notice how after a while water droplets are appearing near the top of the bottle. Once many have formed, the water droplets near the top start falling down to join the rest of the water at the bottom. This is the water cycle!

THE HOWS AND WHYS

When the sun heats up the water, the water begins to evaporate and turns into a vapor. That vapor rises up and begins to condense near the top of the bottle, which is similar to clouds forming. Once the droplets become too heavy, they fall back to the bottom of the bottle, which is similar to how clouds release their vapor in the form of precipitation, and the water falls back to the Earth.

VARIATION

Do the same activity using a resealable plastic bag, and tape the bag to a sunny window.

THE HOWS AND WHYS

Different liquids have different densities. Heavier liquids, like corn syrup and honey, sink to the bottom while lighter liquids, like rubbing alcohol and vegetable oil, float towards the top. Solid objects have their own densities as well, so when they are added to the liquids, they float or sink to the liquid that has a similar density to theirs.

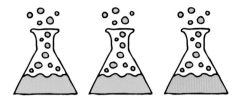

LIQUID DENSITY TOWER

Did you know different liquids have different densities? This means some liquids are heavier than others. Here's a really cool, colorful way to demonstrate those different densities by layering liquids to make a liquid density tower. And for an added effect, try adding some solid objects that will float on the various layers depending on their own densities!

VARIATIONS

Try adding other liquids you can find around the house, such as whole milk and/or dish soap and see where they line up in the tower. Stir the liquids in the tower to see if they mix easily or stay separate. Try adding other solid objects to see whether they float or sink in the tower and which layers they land in.

MATERIALS

- 2 small bowls
- Water*
- Red liquid food coloring
- Rubbing alcohol*
- Green liquid food coloring
- 1 large glass vase or other clear container
- Honey*
- Corn syrup*
- Vegetable oil*
- 1 marble
- 1 cherry tomato
- 1 plastic bead
- 1 ping pong ball

* You need enough of each liquid to create a 1-inch (2.5-cm) layer in your container.

DIRECTIONS

In a small bowl, mix together the water and a few drops of red food coloring. In another small bowl, mix together the rubbing alcohol and a few drops of green food coloring. Slowly add the ingredients to the empty vase in this order: honey, corn syrup, red water, vegetable oil and green rubbing alcohol. Don't worry if the ingredients mix a little, as they should separate in a few seconds.

After all the liquids have been added, you will see the distinct layers. Now you are ready to add your solid objects! Drop in the marble, cherry tomato, plastic bead and ping pong ball, and watch them float and sink to various layers of the tower.

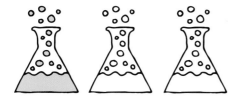

PICK UP AN ICE CUBE WITH SALT AND STRING

Did you know you can pick up an ice cube using salt and a piece of string? It seems impossible, but it's true, and it involves exploring the melting point of water.

MATERIALS

- 1 bowl
- Cold water
- 1 ice cube
- 1 (12-inch [30.5-cm]) piece of thick cotton string
- Coarse sea salt

DIRECTIONS

Fill the bowl nearly to the top with cold water. Place the ice cube in the water and lay the string across the top of the cube. Sprinkle a thin layer of salt on top of the ice cube and string. Wait for about 20 seconds and pick up the string. You will see that the ice cube sticks to the string and is lifted out of the water!

THE HOWS AND WHYS

Salt lowers the melting point of water below 32°F (0°C), which is why we use salt on icy roads in the winter. The salt helps melt the ice on the roads by allowing the ice to melt at lower temperatures. Once the salt is added to the ice cube, a small layer of the cube melts around the string but then refreezes again as the water cools around the string.

VARIATIONS

Try using different kinds of salt to see if one works better. Try lifting 2 ice cubes at once.

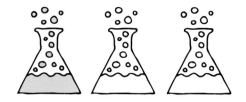

MAKE BUTTER IN A JAR

Did you know you can make homemade butter with just heavy cream, a Mason jar and lots of shaking? It's true! In this simple science experiment, you will turn heavy cream to butter in mere minutes.

MATERIALS

- 1 Mason or resealable jar (baby food jars work well for little hands)
- Heavy whipping cream

DIRECTIONS

Fill the jar about halfway with heavy whipping cream. Seal the jar completely and start shaking. You will begin to notice a thicker substance forming after a few minutes. This is whipped cream. Take a small taste if you want. Keep shaking and soon you will see a thicker substance starting to form along with a liquid. The thicker substance is butter and the liquid is buttermilk. Open the jar at various points and pour out the buttermilk. Keep shaking until the buttermilk stops forming. At this point your butter is complete! Now you can spread it on some bread and enjoy! You can also keep the buttermilk you made (it will stay fresh for 2 to 3 days) and use it to bake.

THE HOWS AND WHYS

Milk consists of liquids and fats. When it is shaken, the solids and liquids separate and the solids stick to each other forming butter (a high-fat substance), and the liquid left forms buttermilk (a low-fat substance).

VARIATIONS

Add a little salt to your butter for some additional flavor. Try making butter with an electric mixer (with an adult's assistance) to see how much faster it forms.

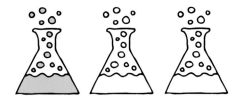

LAVA LAMPS

Lava lamps are so mesmerizing to watch, and here's a fun way to make them at home using just a few simple ingredients. You will be amazed by this cool experiment!

THE HOWS AND WHYS

The oil and water don't mix because they have different densities and the water is denser than the oil. The food coloring contains water, which is why it falls through the oil and doesn't mix with it. Once the tablet pieces are dropped into the mixture, gas bubbles form and cause the food coloring to mix with the water and the colored water bubbles rise up and fall through the oil, just like a real lava lamp!

MATERIALS

- 2 clear containers
- Vegetable oil
- Water
- Liquid food coloring
- Effervescent antacid tablets (such as Alka-Seltzer)

DIRECTIONS

Fill each container about halfway with vegetable oil. Then fill each about one-quarter full with water. Notice how the water sinks and settles below the vegetable oil. Add about 4 to 5 drops of food coloring to each bottle, and notice how the drops fall through the oil to settle between the water and oil layer. Break the antacid tablet into quarters. Drop 1 piece into each liquid mixture, and watch the eruption of bubbles and color! Once the bubbles stop, add another piece of the tablet and the bubbles will take off again.

VARIATIONS

Use a container that can be sealed, like a water bottle or glass jar, and save the water and oil mixture to use for future lava lamps. You can also fill the remainder of the container with water and seal it permanently for a cool sensory bottle that can be shaken to watch the water and oil mix and settle.

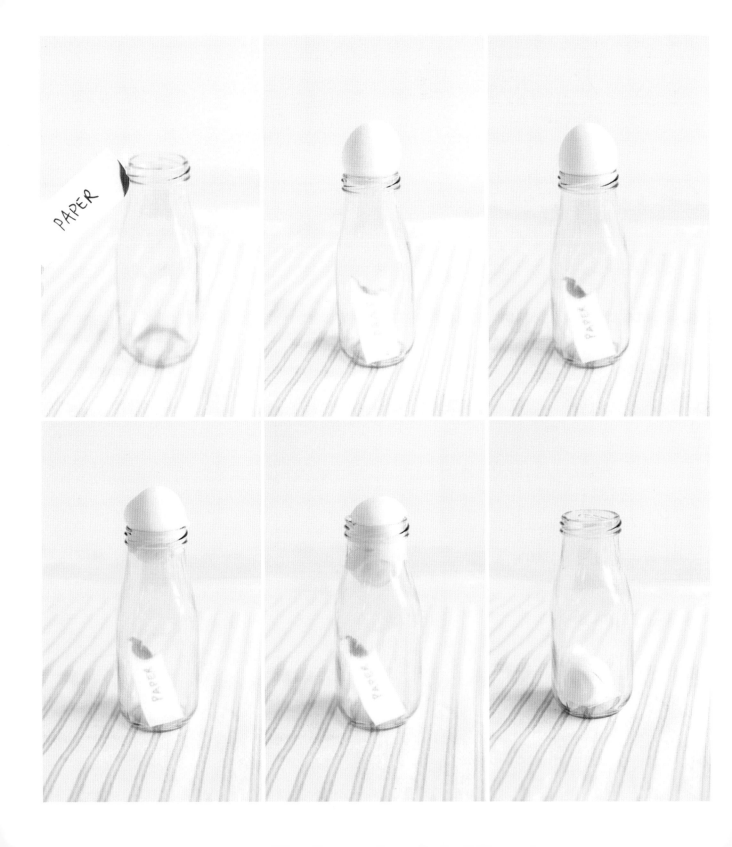

Adult Assistance Required

EGG IN A BOTTLE

This cool science experiment will have both kids and adults amazed as they watch an egg squeeze itself into a bottle seemingly by itself.

THE HOWS AND WHYS

As the fire goes out and the air cools in the bottle, the air contracts and the pressure of the air in the bottle is less than the air outside the bottle. The higher-pressure air outside pushes the egg inside the bottle.

VARIATION

Think of different ways to remove the egg from the bottle. You can use a small spoon or butter knife to cut the egg into pieces and remove the egg.

MATERIALS

- Vegetable oil (optional)
- 1 glass milk bottle (or any glass bottle that has a mouth just smaller than an egg can fit through)
- 1 hard-boiled egg, peeled
- 1 small piece of paper
- A match or lighter (for adult use only)

DIRECTIONS

Add a bit of vegetable oil inside the rim of the bottle. This is not necessary, but it could help the egg fall into the bottle. Place the egg on top of the bottle opening and try pushing it through lightly. It should not be possible to fit the egg into the bottle with light pressure. Remove the egg. Have an adult light the piece of paper on fire and drop it into the glass bottle. Quickly place the egg on top of the bottle opening and watch as the fire fizzles out and the egg squeezes itself into the bottle! Try turning the bottle upside down and see how the egg is now firmly in the bottle.

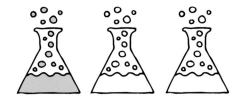

COOKIE PHASES OF THE MOON

The Moon is a beautiful and mysterious body that orbits the Earth and moves through different phases that are repeated every 29.5 days. Using cookies, you can easily recreate these phases!

MATERIALS

- Pen
- Paper
- Chocolate cookies with cream filling (such as Oreos)
- Toothpick

DIRECTIONS

With the pen and paper, create a moon chart and label the phases of the Moon. These phases include a new moon, waxing crescent, first quarter, waxing gibbous, full moon, waning gibbous, last quarter and waning crescent. Separate the cookies so the center cream is exposed. Carve a phase of the Moon in the center cream of 1 cookie with the toothpick. Once you are finished carving the cream center, place your "moon" on the moon chart you created. After you finish all the phases, make sure to show off your creation before you eat it!

THE HOWS AND WHYS

The Moon orbits the Earth, and we are able to view the portion of the Moon that is lit by the sun. The same surface of the Moon always faces the Earth, but the angle of the Sun lighting the Moon changes and gives us the different phases of the Moon. A new moon occurs when the Moon is directly between the Earth and the Sun. A full moon occurs when the Earth is located directly between the Sun and the Moon.

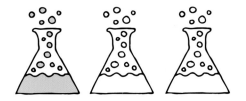

RISING POPCORN

What do you think will happen when you mix popcorn kernels with sugar in a closed bottle? Will they mix together or stay separate? Here's a fun way to demonstrate the tendency of particles of different sizes to separate.

MATERIALS

- Clear bottle or jar with top
- 1–2 cups (200–400 g) sugar (salt or rice would work too)
- ⅓ cup (105 g) popcorn kernels

DIRECTIONS

Fill the bottle or jar about halfway with the sugar. Add the popcorn kernels. Seal the bottle and shake the contents to get them mixed well. Lightly roll the bottle on its side back and forth. You will see the popcorn kernels almost magically rise to the top and separate from the sugar.

THE HOWS AND WHYS

This separation occurs because of a process called particle segregation in which particles of different sizes tend to separate. In this case, the sugar particles are much smaller than the popcorn kernels and therefore they fall between the popcorn kernels and settle on the bottom, making it appear that the popcorn kernels rise to the top.

VARIATION

This experiment can be done with many different materials. Try using golf balls and salt or rocks, pebbles and sand.

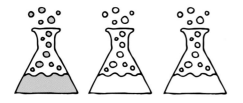

WALKING WATER

Here's a fun and colorful science experiment that demonstrates the concepts of capillary action and transpiration. It's also just super cool to watch the colors travel and mix!

THE HOWS AND WHYS

The water is able to move up and through the paper towel because of a process called capillary action. The water travels up the tiny gaps in the fibers of the paper towel. The water molecules are cohesive so they stay close to each other, but they also bind to the paper towel through a process called adhesion. This process is similar to the way water travels from the roots of plants to the leaves. This process is called transpiration. The gaps within the paper towel act like the capillary tubes of plants and pull the water upwards.

MATERIALS

◦ Water

◦ 6 clear glass or plastic glasses

◦ Red, yellow and blue liquid food coloring

◦ 6 paper towels

DIRECTIONS

Pour water in three of the glasses, until they are about three-quarters full. Add a few drops of food coloring to each glass of water so that you have 1 cup with red water, 1 cup with yellow water and 1 cup with blue water. Arrange the cups in a circle alternating 1 cup with water and 1 empty cup.

Fold each paper towel in half and then in half again vertically to make long strips. Place one end of a strip in an empty glass and the other end in a glass filled with water. Take the next strip and place it in the same glass of water, and then place the other end in an empty glass. Repeat until all of the glasses are linked to each other by paper towel strips. Notice how the paper towel strips immediately start absorbing the water. Wait several hours or overnight and see what happens! The water will move from the full cups to the empty cups and mix to form new colors and create a rainbow of colors!

VARIATION

Make other color combinations using the food coloring and mix them by having them "walk" through the paper towels. Can you make teal, brown or lime green?

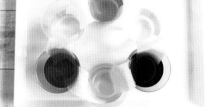

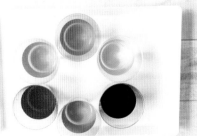

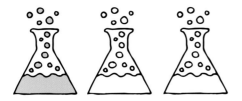

DANCING GRAPES

This experiment will have everyone amazed as the grapes dance through the water, and it is a great introduction to the concept of buoyancy.

MATERIALS

- Seltzer water
- 1 glass vase or jar
- Several grapes

DIRECTIONS

Pour the seltzer water into the vase until it is three-quarters full. Toss in a handful of grapes. Wait a few seconds, and watch as the grapes sink to the bottom, and then as the bubbles attach to the grapes, they start rising up to the top of the water. Once the grapes reach the top, they will bounce around then sink back to the bottom. This "dance" will continue for quite a while, or until most of the bubbles are gone!

THE HOWS AND WHYS

Why do the grapes "dance"? This is a lesson on buoyancy, which is the measure of how something floats or sinks in water or other fluids. The grapes are slightly heavier than the water so they naturally sink to the bottom, but the carbon dioxide bubbles attach to the grapes, causing them to rise to the top. Once the grapes reach the top, the bubbles pop, and the grapes sink back to the bottom where more bubbles attach to them and the process repeats.

VARIATION

Try using raisins, unpopped popcorn kernels or gummy worms instead of grapes to see if you can get them "dancing" as well!

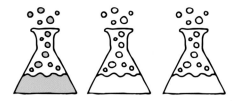

STATIC SPINNING PENCIL

This simple experiment is a great way to show how static electricity can create objects that are positively or negatively charged and once charged, seem to magically move each other! In this experiment you will charge a balloon and then get it to spin a pencil without ever touching the pencil.

MATERIALS

- 1 latex balloon
- 1 pencil
- 1 water bottle full of water, with lid

DIRECTIONS

Blow up the balloon. Balance the pencil horizontally on top of the bottle of water. Rub the balloon against a piece of clothing. Hold the balloon up to one end of the pencil and watch the pencil start spinning.

THE HOWS AND WHYS

When the balloon is rubbed against a piece of clothing, electrons and protons are exchanged and the balloon becomes negatively charged as some of the negative electrons come off the clothing and stick to the balloon. Once the balloon is charged with negative electrons, it attracts the pencil, which is positively charged, and causes the pencil to spin. This is similar to how magnets work.

VARIATIONS

Try the same experiment with a straw instead of a pencil. Try rolling an empty can along the ground using a charged balloon.

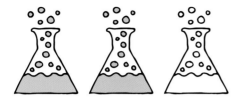

ORANGE PEEL BALLOON POP

Did you know that you can make a balloon pop with an orange peel? It almost sounds unbelievable, but it's true!

MATERIALS

- 1 latex balloon (small water balloons work best)
- 1 orange peel, at least 1 x 2 inches (2.5 x 5 cm)

DIRECTIONS

Blow up the balloon. Hold it close to the orange peel. Squeeze the orange peel next to the balloon and watch what happens. The balloon pops!

THE HOWS AND WHYS

The peel of an orange contains limonene, which is a hydrocarbon. Balloons are made of latex, also a hydrocarbon. Hydrocarbons are non-polar substances, and non-polar substances dissolve well in other non-polar substances. So when the juice from the orange hits the balloon, it dissolves some of the rubber and pops the balloon!

VARIATION

Try doing this experiment with other citrus fruits like lemons, limes or grapefruits.

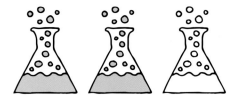

RAINBOW WATER

This experiment is a colorful way to demonstrate water density while creating a rainbow in the water!

MATERIALS

- 6 clear cups or containers
- 3 cups (720 ml) warm water
- Red, yellow and blue liquid food coloring
- 5 tbsp (75 g) white granulated sugar
- 5 spoons or mixers
- 1 dropper
- 1 tall, thin clear container

DIRECTIONS

Fill each cup with ½ cup (120 ml) of warm water. Using warm water will help the sugar absorb more quickly. Add 1 to 2 drops of food coloring to each cup to just slightly color the water and make colored water in red, orange (1 drop red, 1 drop yellow), yellow, green (1 drop yellow, 1 drop blue), blue and purple (1 drop blue, 1 drop red). This experiment works better when the water is only lightly colored.

Add sugar to each of the cups as follows:

Red cup	None
Orange cup	1 tsp (5 g)
Yellow cup	2 tsp (10 g)
Green cup	3 tsp (15 g)
Blue cup	4 tsp (20 g)
Purple cup	5 tsp (25 g)

Stir the water in the cups until all the sugar is dissolved. Make sure to use a different spoon for each cup.

To create the rainbow, use the dropper to add some of the purple liquid to the tall, thin container. Depending on the size of the cup you will want to add 1 to 3 droppers full. Slowly add the blue liquid to the container by taking the dropper and placing it close to the surface of the purple liquid and applying it to the wall of the container. Continue with the green, yellow, orange and red. Make sure you are in a well-lit room or hold the container full of all the colors up to a light or window and see the rainbow of colors in the container.

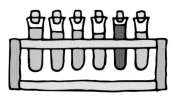

THE HOWS AND WHYS

Adding sugar to the water increases the density of the water, which allows the colors to stay separate. Since the purple water has the most sugar in it, it is the heaviest and stays on the bottom. The red water has no sugar in it, making it the lightest and keeping it on top.

VARIATION

See if you can identify any new colors created when adding the colored water to the tower.

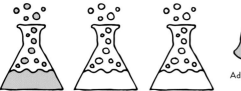

Adult Assistance Required

COLORED FLOWERS

Did you know plants "drink" water too? They do it by absorbing water through their roots in a process called transpiration. This science experiment demonstrates transpiration by showing how colored water moves through the stems of flowers to give them their color.

THE HOWS AND WHYS

The flower petals change color because the tiny tubes (xylem) in the plant drink up the water just like a straw. This process of water moving through a plant to its leaves, stems and flowers is called transpiration. Examine the flower to see if you can see any of the capillaries in the stem and if they match the color of the water they were in.

MATERIALS

◦ Water
◦ Several thin vases or jars
◦ Liquid food coloring
◦ Scissors
◦ White carnations, white roses or daisies
◦ Ruler

DIRECTIONS

Pour the water into the vases until they are one-quarter full. Add a generous amount of different colors of food coloring to each vase. (You want the water to be very saturated with color.) Have an adult cut the bottom of the stems of the flowers at an angle and add one to each of the vases of colored water. Use a ruler to keep the stems shorter than 10 inches (25 cm) so the colored water doesn't have far to travel. It will take about 24 hours for the color to fully absorb, but start checking every few hours to see if the flowers are changing color. Red, blue and black food coloring work best, but test other colors too. Try splitting the flower stem and placing each half of the stem in separate colors. What happens to the flowers?

VARIATION

Try using celery stalks instead of flowers. Take a look at the capillaries of the stalks after they have absorbed the colored water.

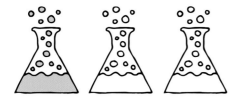

POUR WATER DOWN A STRING

This cool experiment explores the properties of water, including cohesion (water sticks to itself) and adhesion (water sticks to other things). When water is poured down a string, it amazingly sticks to the string as it flows from high to low! This activity can get a bit messy so doing it over a sink is recommended.

MATERIALS

- Water
- 2 cups
- 12-inch (30.5-cm) piece of thick cotton string
- Masking tape

DIRECTIONS

Pour water into one of the cups until it is about three-quarters full. Soak the string in the water until it is fully wet. Remove the string from the water and tape one end of the string to the insides of each cup. Make sure the inside of the cup with water in it is dry where the tape is being applied or it will not stick. Place the empty cup on a table. Raise the cup of water up and slowly pour a small stream of water. Watch it cling to the string and drip off the end into the empty cup.

THE HOWS AND WHYS

Water is made up of 1 oxygen atom and 2 hydrogen atoms. These atoms have positive and negative charges, which causes them to stick together. Water displays properties of both cohesion and adhesion. Cohesion causes the water molecules to stick to themselves and adhesion causes the molecules to stick to other objects. When the water is poured down the string, adhesion causes the water to stick to the string and cohesion causes the water to stick to itself so a stream of water makes its way down the string and into the other cup.

VARIATIONS

Add food coloring to the water for a fun effect. Try using a longer string to see how far you can get the water to travel down the string.

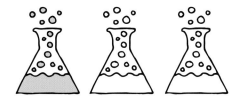

MAGIC PEPPER EXPERIMENT

This simple experiment explores what happens when you change the surface tension of water.

MATERIALS

- 1 large, shallow bowl
- Water
- Black pepper flakes
- Dish soap

DIRECTIONS

Fill the bowl about halfway with water. Sprinkle some pepper flakes on the surface of the water so that it lightly covers the surface. Dip your finger into a bit of dish soap and touch your finger to the water. Watch as the flakes instantly move to the edge of the bowl.

THE HOWS AND WHYS

Water molecules stick together and create surface tension, which causes the surface of the water to bulge up a bit. The pepper flakes float evenly on the surface of the water until dish soap is added. The dish soap lowers the surface tension of the water, so when it is added to the water, the water wants to spread out and it flattens in the bowl, carrying the pepper flakes to the edge.

VARIATION

Use glitter or other spices. Do they work as well as the pepper flakes?

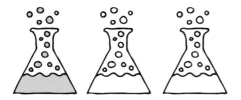

MAGIC MOVING BALL

In this activity you will lift a ball off the table without touching it. Think it's impossible? Well, it's actually very possible and simple to do due to centrifugal force.

MATERIALS

- 1 ping pong ball
- 1 plastic wine glass or other cup or glass that curves inward at the top

DIRECTIONS

Place the ping pong ball on a table. Turn the glass upside down and place it over the ball. Start swirling the ball, rotating the glass in tight circles. As the ball moves around the glass, try lifting the glass off the table. Keep swirling the ball in the glass as you lift, and you will see the ball rise up with the glass as it swirls around the inside. This might take some practice, but don't give up!

THE HOWS AND WHYS

The ball stays in the glass due to centrifugal force, which is the tendency of an object to push outwards when it's moving in a circular motion. As the ball moves in a circle around the glass, it pushes outwards on the glass and seemingly sticks to the wall of the glass, allowing it to lift as the glass rises.

VARIATION

Pour water into a bucket with a handle until it is around one-quarter full. Quickly swing the bucket in a large circle so that it turns completely upside down. Did the water fall out? Unless you stopped your bucket when it was upside down, the water stayed in the bucket without spilling a drop. This is also due to centrifugal force. What other examples of centrifugal force do we see in our everyday lives?

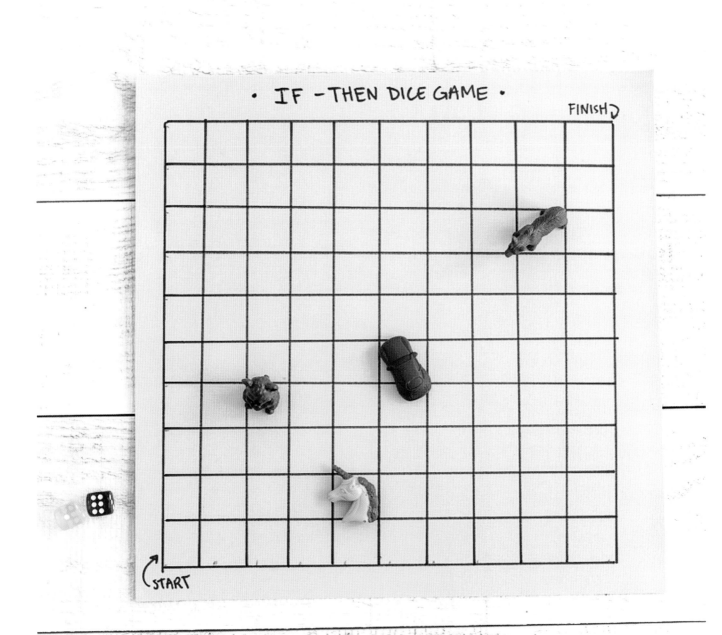

2

ACHIEVABLE TECHNOLOGY IDEAS

When one thinks of technology, our thoughts usually turn right to computers, tablets and smartphones. And while these devices are typically a central part of our lives, this chapter is going to focus on non-screen activities that will introduce you to concepts you will need to master to become a successful coder, should that be something that sparks your interest. There are many skills needed to master coding and kids as young as 2 or 3 can start building a foundation with these activities. Skills such as sequencing (arranging things in a particular order), debugging (identifying mistakes in a process or calculation) and computational thinking (problem-solving in a way a computer could understand) are all incorporated into fun activities that kids of all ages can participate in.

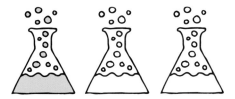

CRACK THE CODE SCAVENGER HUNT

Here's a fun way to incorporate pre-coding and math skills into a fun scavenger hunt for 2 or more players.

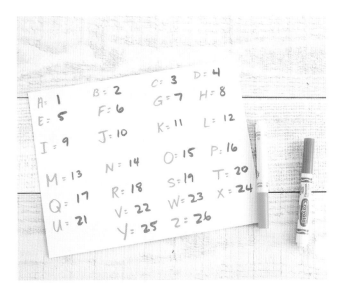

MATERIALS

° Markers, pen or pencil
° Paper
° 2 or more players
° Small prize like a snack or piece of candy

DIRECTIONS

Decide who will be making the scavenger hunt and who will be participating. A parent can help set up the hunt so all the kids playing can participate in decoding and finding the clues. Create a decoding key by assigning each letter in the alphabet a number value, like A=1, B=2, etc. Make sure each player has a key—or make sure everyone shares the one key. Determine 8 to 10 locations where you will hide your clues.

To set up the scavenger hunt, take 8 to 10 small pieces of paper, which will be your clues. On paper #1 draw a horizontal line for each letter of the first location in your scavenger hunt. For example, if there's a clue under a *tree*, draw 4 lines and below each line include the corresponding number on your decoding key for the letters "t," "r," "e" and "e."

Continue making these clues on each piece of paper. Place clue #1 at the starting point of the hunt. This clue will direct players to clue #2, and so on. Once all the clues have been hidden, the participants can start with clue #1 and with the decoding key, they go from there. Once they solve all the clues, have a fun surprise like a snack or piece of candy waiting at the end of the scavenger hunt.

THE HOWS AND WHYS

Challenges like this are great for building problem-solving skills and getting familiar with pre-coding concepts like sequencing (putting things in a particular order) and debugging (correcting errors if their decoding seems incorrect).

VARIATION

For older kids, make the clues math problems like addition, subtraction, multiplication or division, depending on age and skill level.

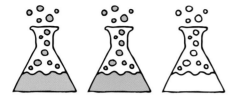

PAINT YOUR NAME IN BINARY CODE

This activity is a great introduction to coding as it teaches the concept of binary code. Binary code is a system of coding involving two symbols, usually 0 and 1. It is the way computers convert and store data. In this activity you'll create a beautiful piece of art while learning this important concept.

THE HOWS AND WHYS

Every computer we use today stores and processes data using binary code. This code allows us to communicate with computers and process the instructions we give them. Although we may type our requests using letters and numbers, those requests are then converted to binary code so the computers can understand and process them.

MATERIALS

- Pencil
- Paper
- Paintbrush
- Watercolor or washable tempera paints

DIRECTIONS

Using the binary conversion chart (see below), lightly pencil the binary code for each letter of your name on the paper. Then using the paintbrush and paint, paint over your pencil drawing to create a final version. Use different colors for each letter of your name or the same for all—it's all about being creative! When the painting is complete, you will have your own unique name painting spelled out in binary code!

Letter	Binary Code	Letter	Binary Code
A	1000001	N	1001110
B	1000010	O	1001111
C	1000011	P	1010000
D	1000100	Q	1010001
E	1000101	R	1010010
F	1000110	S	1010011
G	1000111	T	1010100
H	1001000	U	1010101
I	1001001	V	1010110
J	1001010	W	1010111
K	1001011	X	1011000
L	1001100	Y	1011001
M	1001101	Z	1011010

VARIATION

Try writing secret messages in binary code and have others decode the messages.

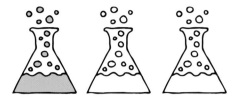

TEACH THE ROBOT CHALLENGE

When learning the concepts of coding, one important aspect is figuring out how many steps are required to perform a simple task. In this activity for 2 players, the challenge is to teach a robot how to do a simple task like making a sandwich.

MATERIALS

- Pencil
- Paper

DIRECTIONS

Start by selecting a simple task like making a sandwich. Write down all the steps needed in order to make a sandwich for an imaginary robot from start to finish. Make sure you have designated a starting point for the robot and are including all instructions like "Walk ten steps to the refrigerator," "Open the refrigerator door with your right hand" and "Reach into the refrigerator with your right hand and remove the lettuce, mayonnaise, lunchmeat and bread from the refrigerator." You can see there are many steps just to start collecting the ingredients for the sandwich. Once the instructions have been completed, have a friend play the robot and try to complete the task.

THE HOWS AND WHYS

Computers do not think for themselves, so we need to tell them exactly what we want them to do when writing computer code. A simple task may sometimes have hundreds of steps to complete and if we leave out just one step, the task will not be completed correctly.

VARIATION

Try coming up with other tasks, write out the steps and have a friend play robot to see if your task is completed correctly.

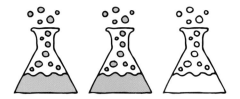

IF-THEN DICE GRID GAME

Here's a fun game that's simple to set up and will teach you the important concept of an if–then statement. An if–then command is a conditional command in programming and it works like this: If a condition is true, then do this command. In this game for 2 or more, players will try to get from the starting point of the grid to the end by rolling a dice and performing commands based on their dice roll.

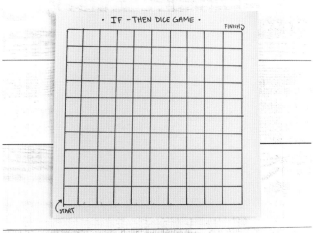

MATERIALS

◦ Pencil
◦ Ruler
◦ Paper
◦ Game pieces of your choice
◦ 1 die
◦ 2 or more players

DIRECTIONS

With the pencil and ruler, have one player draw 10 equally spaced vertical lines on the paper (about ¾ inch [2 cm] apart), and then cross them with 10 equally spaced horizontal lines. In the lower left corner of the 10 x 10 grid, label that box the starting point and in the upper right corner, label that box the finish line. Create rules for how players will move through the game. For example:

• If you roll a 1, then move up 1 space

• If you roll a 2, then move 1 space to the left or right

• If you roll a 3, then move 1 space diagonally in any direction

• If you roll a 4, then move down 1 space

• If you roll a 5, then move up 2 spaces

• If you roll a 6, then move down 2 spaces

(You can make your rules different or use these.)

If a player is unable to make the move due to being at the edge of the board, then the turn goes to the next player. The first player to land their piece in the finish box wins!

Add obstacles to some of the cubes on the grid to make the game more challenging. For an advanced challenge, utilize the concept of "if–then–else" by only having commands for rolls from 1 to 4 of the dice and an "else" statement that says to move up 2 spaces. If the players roll a 5 or 6, they would execute the "else" statement.

Understanding the concept of "IF this condition exists, THEN this command will happen next" is key to beginning to learn how to code.

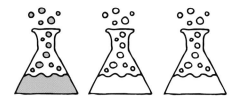

CAMERA NATURE WALK

Getting outdoors is so important for our development and emotional well-being. Here's a fun way to incorporate technology while getting outside and engaging with nature.

MATERIALS

∘ Digital or phone camera

DIRECTIONS

Before leaving for the walk, create a list of some specific items to look for, such as 10 different leaves, 5 insects, 5 things you've never seen before or anything else fun that will keep you on the lookout as you walk. As you spot the items, take pictures of them. At the end of the walk, see how many of the items you found.

THE HOWS AND WHYS

Keeping on the lookout for specific types of things will keep you hyper-aware of your environment on the walk, and documenting your finds in photographs will make for an even more engaging experience. When you look back at all the things you found, you will be proud and amazed that all these things were right outside your front door!

VARIATION

For an additional art project, print out one of the pictures in black and white and color in the picture.

3

EASY ENGINEERING CHALLENGES

Building is something that you've probably done for as long as you can remember. We are all born natural builders and it's fun to build structures not only with blocks, but with unusual items as well, such as paper towel rolls, sticks and rocks. The activities in this chapter encourage critical thinking and problem-solving while building with unconventional tools and objects beyond basic building blocks. You will be challenged to work together to build catapults, ramps, mazes, towers and more! You'll be surprised that many items around the house can be used to build unique structures.

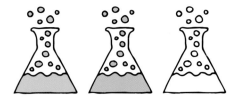

CUP STACKING WITH A RUBBER BAND AND STRING

Have you ever tried making a pyramid with cups using only rubber bands and string? Think it's impossible? Here's a fun challenge that will build engineering, creativity and problem-solving skills and is a great team building activity.

MATERIALS

- 48-inch (122-cm) piece of string
- Ruler
- Scissors
- 1 rubber band
- 10 or more paper or plastic cups
- 2–4 helpers

DIRECTIONS

To create the tool you will use to lift the cups, cut 4 pieces of string about 12 inches (30.5 cm) long. Tie the end of each string to the rubber band, evenly spacing the knots on the rubber band. Place 10 or more cups face down on a table or flat surface. Have each person hold 1 to 2 pieces of string and stretch the rubber band so that it can fit around the plastic cup. Once the rubber band is placed around the plastic cup, release the strings a bit so that the rubber band contracts around the cup. The cup can now be lifted and moved to build the pyramid. Continue with all the cups until the pyramid is completed.

THE HOWS AND WHYS

This activity is great for many reasons, but particularly for the coordination and cooperation needed for the group to work together to build the pyramid. The tool used to lift the cups will not work unless the entire group is working together and communicating. The problem-solving that is needed to figure out how best to operate the lifting tool is also an important skill to develop.

VARIATIONS

If you have enough people, create 2 or more teams and see who can complete the pyramid the fastest. Try the challenge without anyone talking to see how this changes the group dynamic.

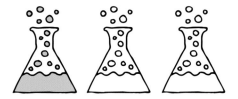

ROLLED-UP PAPER AND TAPE STRUCTURES

Open-ended challenges are awesome because they allow you to use your creativity and problem-solving skills to come up with solutions. In this activity you are challenged to build the tallest structure possible using only paper and tape.

MATERIALS

- Several pieces of newspaper or other type of paper
- Masking tape

DIRECTIONS

Roll 1 piece of paper diagonally starting from one corner. Keep rolling until the entire sheet is rolled up. Your piece of paper should look like a long, skinny tube. Secure the other corner to the roll with tape. Make several of these rolls and tape them together to build as tall of a structure as possible. You can use tape to secure the rolls to each other. Make it a competition or team activity to see who can build the tallest structure. What shapes make the most secure structures? Triangles? Squares?

THE HOWS AND WHYS

This is a great activity for learning about structures and which shapes support the most weight and allow the structures to stand strong without falling.

VARIATION

Try building a fort that is large enough for someone to fit inside.

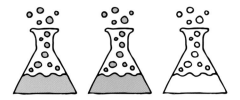

WALL PIPE MAZE

I always save our empty paper towel and toilet paper rolls as there are just so many creative ways to use them. This activity challenges you to create a maze on the wall using just tape and paper rolls.

MATERIALS

- Empty paper towel and toilet paper rolls
- Painter's tape
- A clear wall you can place tape on
- 1 small ball or marble
- 1 cup

DIRECTIONS

Using all the empty paper rolls, start high on a wall and tape the rolls to the wall in a way that will allow a small ball to move from one roll to the next all the way down the wall and land in a cup at the bottom. Once you have the maze built, drop the ball down the maze. Does it make it to the bottom? If not, adjust the rolls and try again. Keep making adjustments until the maze works perfectly!

THE HOWS AND WHYS

Gravity is a force that attracts objects toward each other. It is gravitational forces that keep us planted on Earth, and gravity is what causes the marble to roll down the maze toward the ground.

VARIATIONS

To double the number of rolls you have, cut them in half lengthwise and use half so they are open on the top, and you will have twice as many rolls for your maze. Try building the maze on a corner wall and see if you can get the ball to move from one wall to the other and back again.

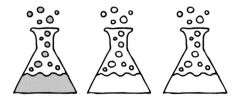

CARDBOARD AND CLOTHESPIN MARBLE RUN

Marble runs are mesmerizing to watch but usually involve spending hours putting together a toy with several hundred pieces. This activity takes only minutes to set up and is just as fun to watch, adjust and build!

MATERIALS

○ 2 x 12–inch (5 x 30.5–cm) cardboard strip
○ 20–25 clothespins
○ 1 marble

DIRECTIONS

Clip the clothespins to the sides of the cardboard strip at 20-degree angles (see project photo). The clothespins should be arranged so that they zig-zag and are never directly across from each other. Once you have all your clothespins attached, lift one end of the cardboard up at an angle. Release the marble down the maze. The marble will bounce back and forth between the clothespins as it moves down the maze. If the marble falls off the maze, adjust the clothespin angles and distance from the other clothespins and test to see if the marble stays on the maze after the adjustments have been made. Keep testing and adjusting until the marble makes it to the end of the maze. Adjust the angle of the maze so that it is steeper. Does the marble fall faster?

THE HOWS AND WHYS

This is a great problem-solving activity as you will find the marble falls off the maze if the clothespins are too far apart or not at the correct angle. It's also a lesson in gravity as the marble will fall faster when one end of the maze is lifted higher.

VARIATION

For an additional challenge, try using several pieces of cardboard and some objects to prop up the maze and see if you can get the maze to turn in different directions.

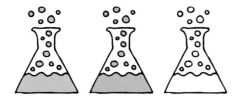

CRAFT STICK CATAPULT

Catapults are a great way to learn the concepts of physics and motion. In addition to building the catapult, you can test launching various items and hypothesize on which items will go the farthest.

THE HOWS AND WHYS

There are some great lessons on physics, motion and energy in this activity. When the arm of the catapult is pulled back, a large amount of potential energy is stored, and then when the arm is released, the energy is converted into kinetic energy, causing the object sitting on the spoon to launch into the air. But why doesn't the object continue to fly forever once it leaves the catapult? That is because of gravity, which causes the flying objects to make an arc that eventually causes them to fall back to the ground.

MATERIALS

- 12 craft sticks
- 7 rubber bands
- 1 plastic spoon
- Items to launch, such as pompoms, marshmallows, cotton balls and anything you can find around the house
- Ruler

DIRECTIONS

Stack 10 craft sticks together and apply 1 rubber band to each end of the group to hold them together. Stack the 2 remaining sticks together and apply a rubber band on one end. Separate the open end of the group of 2 sticks and place the large group in between them. Use 2 more rubber bands to secure the large group to the upper stick in a crisscross pattern. Finally, place the spoon on the upper stick, secure with 2 rubber bands and let the fun begin! Try launching various projectiles and measuring the distances the various objects are able to travel in the air using the ruler.

VARIATIONS

Launch the same object 10 times and see if the distance changes based on how far the launch arm is held down. Try launching some unusual objects such as a feather, a grape or an eraser. Try making the arm of the catapult longer by using another rubber band to add another craft stick to the arm. Does this change how far the catapult launches projectiles?

STACKABLE CHIPS RING CHALLENGE

Stackable potato chips, such as Pringles, have a unique shape and curvature that allows them to be stacked into the shape of a perfect ring! This activity takes absolutely no time to set up but I gave it a difficulty rating of 3 as it is challenging to solve and takes patience and perseverance.

MATERIALS

- 1–2 tubes of stackable chips, such as Pringles (I recommend original flavor as you don't want lots of flavor powder getting everywhere.)
- Silicone mat or other nonslip surface (optional)

DIRECTIONS

Place 2 chips next to each other horizontally on the mat. Make sure that the longer edges touch the mat and the rest of the chip is in the air. Place another chip centered between them, directly on top of them. This is the foundation for your ring. Continue placing chips in the same direction to form a full circle. There is a lot of problem-solving and trial and error involved in this challenge, but it is possible to do and you will feel so great once you complete the challenge!

Tip: Create a base with quite a few layers before trying to build the sides and top of the ring. Your final ring will be very thick on the bottom, much thinner on the sides and only 1 to 2 layers on the top.

THE HOWS AND WHYS

There are a few concepts to cover as to how this ring is possible. The chips are able to stack without falling if the center of mass of the top chip doesn't fall over the edge of the chip below it. When the chips start getting vertical on the sides of the ring, frictional forces play a role in keeping the ring up. The frictional forces on both sides of the chips help overcome the forces of gravity and keep the chips vertically standing.

VARIATION

What other structures can you make with the chips? A boat? A bridge?

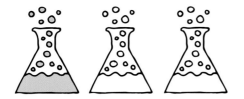

ALPHABET TREE CHALLENGE

This activity is inspired by one of my all-time favorite children's books, *Chicka Chicka Boom Boom* **by Bill Martin Jr. and John Archambault. The book is about how all the letters decide to meet at the top of a coconut tree. In this activity, the challenge is to build a tree and balance as many letters as possible on the top of the tree.**

MATERIALS

- 1 empty toilet paper roll
- 4 craft sticks (I used green to represent the leaves on a tree.)
- Magnetic letters (The magnets aren't necessary for the activity, but they give the letters a bit more weight, which allows the structure to tip if it's not balanced properly.)

DIRECTIONS

Balance the craft sticks on top of the toilet paper roll to make your tree. Start placing letters on the top of the tree, one at a time. Be careful to place the letters in a way that they stay balanced or the sticks will fall off and you'll have to start over. Count how many letters you are able to get to balance on the tree before it falls. See if you can get all the letters to stay balanced on the tree without falling off.

THE HOWS AND WHYS

If the letters are placed in such a way that it causes the center of gravity to shift past the point where the sticks are touching the toilet paper roll, the sticks will tip and fall off the tree. Keeping equal weight distribution on the sticks is the key to being successful in this challenge.

VARIATIONS

For an additional challenge, try lifting the tree off the ground once all the letters are placed on it. You could also do the challenge with small objects like pompoms.

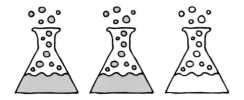

FLOATING BALL EXPERIMENT

Here is a fun experiment that will allow a small ball to seemingly float in the air due to changes in air pressure.

THE HOWS AND WHYS

The reason the ball floats is based on Bernoulli's principle, which is the same principle that is what allows airplanes to fly. Bernoulli's principle states that the faster air flows over an object, the less the air pushes on that object's surface. As you blow air on the ball through the straw, it lowers the air pressure around the ball and keeps it in the air. The ball is trying to escape the blowing air, but since this air is at a lower pressure, the higher pressure air on either side forces it back into the lower pressure area (the moving air).

MATERIALS

- Scissors
- 1 paper plate (or small, round piece of paper)
- Tape
- 1 bendy straw
- 1 pompom
- Aluminum foil

DIRECTIONS

Cut a straight line from the outside to the center of the paper plate. Fold the edges of the plate together to create a cone shape. Secure the cone with tape. Cut a very small hole in the tip of the cone and insert the small end of the straw. Secure the straw to the cone with tape and be sure the hole is fully covered with tape.

To create the ball, wrap the pompom with a small piece of aluminum foil so that it is fully covered. Place the ball in the cone and blow slowly but firmly into the straw. Be sure the straw is pointed straight up to the sky and you will see the ball float in the cone or slightly above as the air seems to move around it.

VARIATIONS

Another way to demonstrate Bernoulli's principle is by using a hair dryer. With an adult's help, point the hair dryer up to the sky, turn it on in cool air mode and place a ping pong ball in the air stream. The ping pong ball will float above the hair dryer but not blow away.

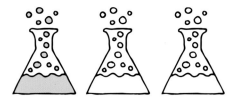

3-D CRAFT STICK ART

The challenge in this activity is to build 3-D art structures using only clothespins, binder clips and colored craft sticks. It is open-ended and the only requirement is that it's sturdy enough to be able to stand up.

MATERIALS

- 10 or more clothespins
- 10 or more binder clips
- 30 or more colored craft sticks

DIRECTIONS

Build anything you want using the clothespins, binder clips and craft sticks. If you need some inspiration or ideas to build, you can build flowers, 3-D shapes, towers and bridges to name a few things. Use the clothespins and binder clips to hold the structures together and help them stand up.

THE HOWS AND WHYS

An important part of STEAM activities is allowing yourself to be creative and problem solve. This is a great open-ended activity that will allow you to do just that and come up with some creative and beautiful works of art.

VARIATIONS

Add googly eyes to your structures to make them come alive. Try building bridges, and if you have enough people to make 2 teams, see which team's bridge can support the most weight.

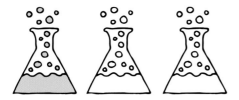

STOMP AND CATCH

These stomp and catch boards are so fun to play with and can teach some important lessons about physics.

THE HOWS AND WHYS

Stomping on the board sets the board and the bag in motion. When the end of the board hits the ground, it stops the board from moving, but the bag stays in motion as nothing is stopping it from moving. This is the concept of inertia. Inertia states that an object in motion will stay in motion until it meets an external force. In this case, the bag will stay in motion until you catch it, or until gravity causes it to stop rising into the sky and pulls it back down to the ground.

MATERIALS

- 1 sturdy, rectangular board, such as a large cutting board or a wooden plank
- 1 small, cylindrical object, such as an empty stackable chip can
- 1 small, lightweight beanbag or individual package of crackers

DIRECTIONS

Place the board flat on the ground. Place the cylindrical object under one end of the board, about one third from the edge. Place the small bean bag on top of the opposite end of the board that the cylindrical object is under. Stomp on the end of the board that is sticking up. This will cause the small bag to fly up into the air. Try to catch the bag as it flies into the air.

VARIATION

Look for other objects to launch off your board. Which objects launch the highest?

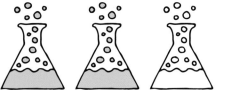

Adult Assistance Required

POMPOM SHOOTERS

These pompom shooters are simple to build and you will have hours of fun launching various small objects!

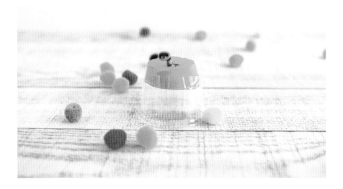

THE HOWS AND WHYS

When the balloon is pulled back before launch, it has a high level of potential energy. Once the balloon is released, that potential energy is converted to kinetic energy and the pompom is launched out of the shooter. The pompom continues to move until gravity gradually causes it to fall to the ground.

MATERIALS

- 1 latex balloon
- Scissors
- 1 clear plastic cup
- Clear packing tape
- Several pompoms, marshmallows, foil balls or ping pong balls

DIRECTIONS

Tie a knot in the bottom of the balloon. Cut the top tip of the balloon off. Have an adult help you cut off the bottom of the plastic cup. Stretch the open end of the balloon over the bottom of the plastic cup. Use the clear tape to secure the balloon to the cup. Your shooter is ready to launch. Drop a pompom into the cup, pull the knot of the balloon back and let it go to launch the pompom into the air.

VARIATIONS

Find other small objects around the house to launch. Try jumbo marshmallows versus standard and mini-marshmallows. Which ones go the farthest? Have a competition to see who can launch an object the farthest. Try launching the same object 10 times. Does it go the same distance every time? Try pulling the balloon back various lengths to launch. Does it affect how far the pompom travels?

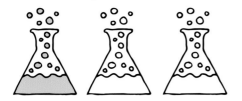

CREPE PAPER NINJA MAZE

Building mazes and then trying to navigate through them is excellent for building creativity and problem-solving skills. In this fun activity, you will build a life-size maze and pretend you're a ninja trying to navigate through it.

MATERIALS

• 3 rolls of crepe paper
• 1 roll of 1-inch (2.5-cm)-thick painter's tape

DIRECTIONS

Find a hallway or a part of the house that has two walls that are 3 to 4 feet (91 to 122 cm) apart for a length of about 6 to 10 feet (183 to 305 cm). Tape the end of a roll of crepe paper to the wall and then unroll the paper and tape it to the other wall. Keep going back and forth between the walls, taping the crepe paper at various heights so there are barriers at high, medium and low levels of the wall. Continue until the roll is complete. Then start with a second and third roll until you've completed your maze. Your goal is to navigate through the maze without knocking down any of the crepe paper!

THE HOWS AND WHYS

The maze is sturdy, but if enough pressure is applied to one of the strips of crepe paper, the force will eventually cause it to fall from the wall or rip.

VARIATION

Once you are able to make it through the maze without knocking down any of the crepe paper, try navigating the maze without touching the crepe paper.

4

ACCESSIBLE ART PROJECTS

Art brings beauty into our world and is such an important component of any design. As a future scientist, engineer or maybe even mathematician, you also want to keep design in the forefront of your mind as you innovate and create our future world. These fun, simple art activities will help you create amazing works of art all while learning about important STEAM concepts!

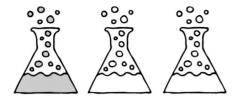

DRAWING PORTRAITS ON SHEET PROTECTORS

This hilariously fun art project is an excellent partner activity that is guaranteed to garner lots of laughs! It is also great for studying facial features and the relationship and symmetry between features.

MATERIALS

- 2 participants
- 2 clear, plastic sheet protectors (Stiff ones that hold their shape as you don't want flimsy ones that will wrap around the face.)
- Dry-erase markers (Washable paint would also work but would be messier.)
- White surface or white paper
- Ruler

DIRECTIONS

Have one person hold a sheet protector in front of their face. Have a second person attempt to draw their face using the dry-erase markers. After the drawing is complete, have them switch roles so the other person can draw. Place the sheet protectors against a white surface or put a sheet of white paper in each sheet protector to view the final result. Take some measurements of the facial features such as the distance between the eyes, the distance between the nose and the mouth, etc. How do those distances differ between the two portraits?

THE HOWS AND WHYS

We are all unique and have our own unique face (unless you are an identical twin). As humans, we are highly adept at recognizing each other by how our faces look and what makes them unique. Some faces are more symmetrical than others and some people have larger features (such as eyes, nose, lips) than others. What makes your face special and unique?

VARIATION

Try adapting this activity for a holiday like Halloween and draw monster versions of each other.

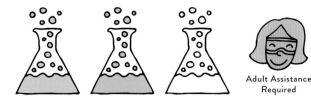

POOL NOODLE AND TOOTHPICK CREATURES

Pool noodles are one of my favorite materials to use for STEAM activities. They are usually available in the spring and summer at any dollar store, so I stock up to have them all year long. Here's a fun art activity using only pool noodles and toothpicks that will get the creative juices flowing and allow you to make colorful 3-D creatures!

MATERIALS

◦ Bread knife (for adult use only)
◦ 3–4 pool noodles in various bright colors
◦ Ruler
◦ Toothpicks

DIRECTIONS

Have your adult cut the pool noodles with the bread knife into shapes of various widths. I suggest a few cylinders that are about 4 inches (10 cm) long to make the bodies and then some that are 1 inch (2.5 cm), 2 inches (5 cm) and 3 inches (8 cm) long for other parts of the bodies. Also cut some of the 1-inch (2.5-cm) circles in half to make semicircles and some into smaller pieces for smaller body parts like ears, hands and feet. Now attach the pool noodle pieces together using the toothpicks to build your pool noodle creatures!

THE HOWS AND WHYS

The toothpicks stick easily into the pool noodles and stay put, allowing for lots of various shapes and structures to easily be built. When you build using only a few materials and very minimal instruction, it allows you to build your creativity skills and you will be surprised at the amazing creations you will come up with!

VARIATION

Try building structures such as buildings with the same materials. How tall can you make a building using only pool noodles and toothpicks? What other creations can you come up with?

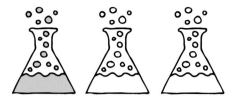

Adult Assistance
Required

RAINBOW PAPER

If I told you that you could make rainbow art out of black construction paper with a drop of clear nail polish, would you believe me? Well, it's true and this activity shows you exactly how to do it!

THE HOWS AND WHYS

The rainbow colors appear because of a natural phenomenon called thin-film interference. It is when the upper and lower boundaries of a thin film (aka the nail polish on the paper) get in the way of each other and either amplify or reduce the light that is reflected. It is the same phenomenon that sometimes causes us to see rainbows in soap bubbles, oil on the sidewalk or puddles of water.

MATERIALS

- Black construction paper
- Scissors
- Water
- Small bowl
- Clear nail polish (for adult use only)

DIRECTIONS

Cut the black construction paper into small rectangles or squares (2 to 3 inches [5 to 8 cm]). Have a bunch ready so you can repeat the experiment over and over. Pour water into the bowl until it is three-quarters full. Have an adult drop 1 small drop of clear nail polish into the water and immediately, within 10 seconds, immerse the black paper completely into the water and remove it right away. Set it aside to dry. Repeat by adding another drop of nail polish and dipping a new piece of paper into the water. Once the paper dries, you will see the beautiful dark rainbows that appear on the paper!

VARIATIONS

Try getting the rainbows to appear on soap bubbles or place a small amount of oil on asphalt or dark pavement.

PENCIL TWIST OPTICAL ILLUSION

An optical illusion occurs when our eyes take in an image and our brain processes it but it is not, in reality, what it seems. In this activity you will create your own optical illusion and examine how your brain is getting tricked!

THE HOWS AND WHYS

Our eyes take in so much visual information and our brain tries to process all that information into what is important and meaningful. An optical illusion is something that tricks the brain into thinking it's seeing something that is actually not there.

MATERIALS

- Markers or crayons
- 2 notecards
- 1 pencil
- Tape

DIRECTIONS

Draw a picture on the notecards where some elements are on one card, and other elements are on the other. For example, if you draw a sun, draw the inner circle of the sun on one card, and the sun rays on the other card. Be sure to keep your drawing aligned so that the rays are drawn in the same spot as if they were on the card with the circle. Once you've completed your drawing, place both of the cards back to back so the drawing is facing out on both sides of the cards.

Stick the pencil in between the two cards and tape the cards together and to the pencil to secure them in place. Spin the pencil between your hands so that the notecards move in a circular motion and your eyes are seeing both cards going back and forth. What do you see? You should see the complete sun picture with the center and rays even though they are actually part of two different drawings!

VARIATIONS

Draw a solid black lightbulb shape on a piece of paper. Stare at the lightbulb for about 20 seconds and then quickly look at a white wall. What do you see?

CRAFT STICK COLOR MIXING

There is something so fascinating about taking two colors, mixing them and seeing a new color emerge. It's almost magical! Here's a simple experiment you can do that is mess-free and takes only a minute to set up.

MATERIALS

- 3 clear plastic or glass cups
- Water
- 2 blue craft sticks
- 2 red craft sticks
- 2 yellow craft sticks

DIRECTIONS

Pour the water into each cup until they are three-quarters full. Add 2 colored craft sticks to each cup of water. I recommend the following pairs: red/blue, red/yellow, yellow/blue. Check back on the sticks every few hours and you will notice the clear water turning colors. The red/blue sticks will create purple water. The red/yellow sticks will create orange water. The yellow/blue sticks will create green water.

THE HOWS AND WHYS

The primary colors are red, yellow and blue. If you have those three colors, you can make all the colors of the rainbow just by mixing them. The secondary colors are orange, green and purple. They are a combination of two of the primary colors and are made by mixing equal parts of two primary colors. White, black and gray are not considered true colors but are neutral hues and are used to lighten or darken primary and secondary colors. To make a color lighter, add white. Pink is a combination of red and white. To make a color darker, add black. Maroon is a combination of black and red.

VARIATIONS

Try using candies like Skittles or M&M's to do the color mixing. What happens when you mix all three primary colors?

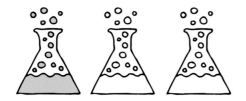

MONSTER BUGS

Process art is when the focus is on the activity of making the art rather than the final outcome. This monster bug painting technique is a super-fun process art activity, and the final results just happen to be amazingly creepy and cool!

MATERIALS

- Water
- Pipette
- Watercolor paper or plain white paper
- Liquid food coloring of different colors
- Black marker

DIRECTIONS

Place 1 large drop of water on the paper with the pipette. Add 1 drop of food coloring to the water drop on the paper. Spread the water from the drop in long sweeps with the pipette to make the legs and tentacles. Repeat this process to make several bugs on your paper. Let the painting dry overnight, and then use a marker to add eyes and a mouth to complete the monster bugs.

THE HOWS AND WHYS

Process art emphasizes viewing art creation as a creative journey and puts emphasis on the techniques and joy of creating the art itself such as color selection, gathering materials, creating patterns and specific movements.

VARIATIONS

Try using different materials, like a fork, to make the legs and tentacles. Do they turn out differently? Try spreading the water to draw actual animals or people.

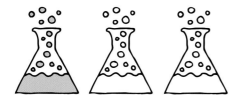

BLOW PAINTING

Blow painting is another fun process art activity that uses your breath to help move the watercolors on the paper to make amazingly beautiful paintings!

THE HOWS AND WHYS

Because there is excess water on the paper, when air is blown on the colored water it splatters away from the straw, creating beautiful patterns and splatter prints.

MATERIALS

- 1 small cup of water
- Paintbrush
- Watercolor paints
- Watercolor paper or plain white paper
- 1 straw

DIRECTIONS

Dip the paintbrush in the cup of water to wet it, and apply some watercolor paint to the brush. Start painting your picture on the paper, and be sure to use a generous amount of water so there is some extra water on your painting. Make a simple drawing like a circle or heart in the middle of the paper and try using 2 to 3 colors that go well together (such as shades of blue/green or blue/purple or red/orange) as they will start to blend. Once you are happy with your initial shape, blow on the painting through the straw. Start from the center of the painting and move outward. Notice the extra watercolor paint on the painting move and make beautiful patterns. Keep turning the paper and blowing until the painting is complete. If the watercolor isn't streaking, add more water over the paint that is already on the paper.

VARIATION

Draw a face with black marker and apply the paint along the hairline. Then use the straw to blow the hair upwards and outwards from the face to create a crazy hair picture.

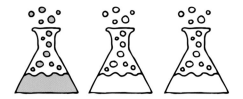

PAPER TOWEL AND MARKER WATERCOLOR PAINTING

Did you know you can use markers and water to make beautiful watercolor paintings? It's true! Here's a simple activity that allows you to create beautiful watercolor paintings without using watercolors!

MATERIALS

- Paper towel
- Washable markers
- 1 dropper
- Water

DIRECTIONS

Draw a picture on the paper towel using washable markers. Once your drawing is complete, fill the dropper with water. Slowly place 5 to 10 drops of water on your painting. You don't want to use too much water, but rather, just enough to allow it to absorb into the paper towel and reach the edges. Add an extra drop or two if you see the edges are still dry after a few minutes. You will see the colors of your picture start to blend together and form a beautiful blended print. Hang to dry or set on a dry surface and allow the paper towel to completely dry.

THE HOWS AND WHYS

Water absorbs easily into a paper towel because of a process called capillary action. This is why you use paper towels to clean up spills! Paper towels are porous and contain small holes throughout that allow the water to absorb and move through those small holes. When you apply color, the water gets colored and transfers some of that color as it spreads through the paper towel.

VARIATIONS

Use clean coffee filters for a similar effect. Once the paper towel is dry, cut it into fun shapes like dinosaurs or hearts and add faces or additional details with a black marker.

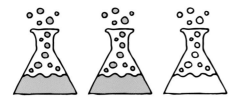

BROOMSTICK DRAWING

Here's a fun process art activity that will have you up on your feet while you create your drawings as you pretend you're using giant markers.

MATERIALS

- Butcher paper or a large roll of paper
- Masking or painter's tape
- Washable markers
- Broomstick or other long stick

DIRECTIONS

Tape a large piece of paper to the floor. Tape a marker to the broomstick so that it is sticking out about 2 inches (5 cm) past the top of the broomstick. Remove the lid of the marker and flip the broomstick over so that the tip of the marker is facing the ground. Use the upside-down broomstick as a big marker and make a drawing on the paper. How different does it feel to draw using such a large and long marker?

THE HOWS AND WHYS

Using conventional items in unconventional ways allows us to challenge our way of thinking and helps build the ability to think outside the box. In this activity, you are taking the very normal activity of drawing a picture with markers and making the markers extremely long. This changes the way you need to position your body to make the drawing as well as how you hold the marker using your hands and arms. Suddenly, making a simple drawing has become an entirely different physical experience!

VARIATIONS

Write your name or play a game of tic-tac-toe with someone.

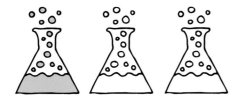

MARBLED PAPER

Marbled patterns are so pretty and seem so difficult and complex to create, but with this simple technique, you can create beautiful marbled prints on paper!

THE HOWS AND WHYS

Marble is created when limestone is exposed to high temperature and pressure. The veins of different colors are often caused by clay or other impurities that are in the limestone before it turns to marble.

VARIATIONS

Make personalized cards with marbled paper you have made or cut out shapes with the marbled paper. Once all the marbled paper is made, put your hands into the remaining shaving cream for a fun, messy, sensory activity.

MATERIALS

- 1 large baking dish
- 1 baking sheet or large tray
- Shaving cream
- 1 spoon or spatula
- Liquid food coloring
- 1 craft stick
- Several pieces of 4 x 4–inch (10 x 10–cm) paper or cardstock
- Paper towels

DIRECTIONS

Place the dish on the baking sheet. Add shaving cream to the dish. Smooth out the surface with the spoon or spatula. Place drops of food coloring on top of the shaving cream. Use a color scheme with 2 to 3 colors or go crazy with all the colors of the rainbow. Mix the colors into the shaving cream with the craft stick.

Then place a piece of paper or cardstock on top of the shaving cream. Lift the paper out, place it on a tray and wipe away the extra shaving cream with the craft stick. Be sure to wipe the shaving cream away right away and don't allow it to sit on the paper for a long time as it will stain the paper and not have the desired effect. Keep lots of paper towels handy. What you have left on the paper is a beautiful marble print.

Let the paper dry completely, which only takes about 10 minutes. Repeat the process with the other side of the paper if you want.

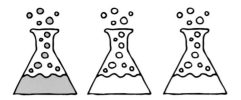

SCRAPE PAINTING

Who says you need a paintbrush to make a painting? In this fun process art activity, you will use only a credit card to make an incredible piece of art!

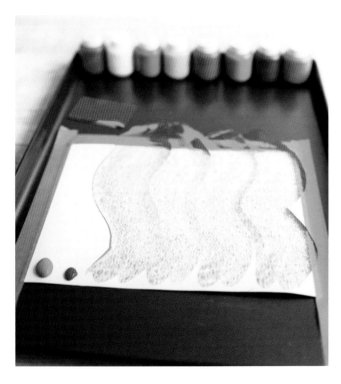

MATERIALS

- Masking tape
- White drawing or other thick paper
- 1 baking sheet
- Washable paint (because it can get messy)
- Credit card or small cardboard square
- Paper towels

DIRECTIONS

Tape 3 sides of the paper to the baking sheet. Don't tape the side where you will place the paint (see photo below). Place a few dollops of paint onto the paper. Use 2 to 3 colors for a more controlled color theme, or use as many colors as possible for a rainbow effect. With the credit card, scrape the dollops of paint in the desired direction to cover the paper. Use paper towels to wipe the credit card after each scrape to help keep the colors separated. Add more paint and keep scraping to fill in any empty spaces until the painting is complete.

VARIATION

Try scrape painting on a larger scale using butcher paper and squeegees!

5

NO PROBLEM MATH ACTIVITIES

Math skills are critically important to master, but require lots of repetition and practice. This means math can sometimes be rather dry and boring. These simple activities will have you counting and practicing math facts without even realizing you are learning!

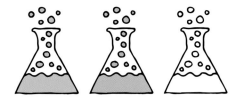

PAPER TOWEL ROLL POMPOM CHALLENGE

Paper towel rolls are one of my favorite recycled materials and can be repurposed in many different ways. For this activity, you will cut them into sections and use them to make a number maze for a pompom to move through.

THE HOWS AND WHYS

The dab of glue on each piece holds the rolls in place in the tray and allows the pompom to move through the maze when the tray is tilted back and forth. The pompom moves freely through the maze because it is not held down.

MATERIALS

- Empty paper towel (or toilet paper) rolls
- Scissors
- Ruler
- Shallow cardboard or plastic tray
- Glue
- Washable marker
- Pompom or small round object

DIRECTIONS

Cut the paper towel rolls into 1½-inch (4-cm) sections. Once you have 10 pieces, arrange them randomly inside the tray. Be sure to leave enough room so the pompom can roll between the pieces. Lift each piece and place a small drop of glue under it. Replace it back in the same spot on the tray. Allow the glue to dry for about 1 hour. Once the glue is dry, write the numbers 1 through 10 on top of the pieces in a random order. Place the pompom in the tray and then the game can begin.

The object of the game is to get the pompom to roll through all the numbered pieces in the correct order. If multiple kids are playing, you can time each child to see who can complete the challenge the fastest.

VARIATIONS

Use something other than numbers to label the rolls. It can be colors of the rainbow, letters or some other pattern of numbers such as counting by 2s, 5s or 10s.

FLOATING LIDS MATH FACTS

Practicing math facts is an important part of becoming a math whiz. Unfortunately, sometimes it can be a somewhat boring process. This activity makes practicing math facts so much fun and it only takes a few minutes to set up.

THE HOWS AND WHYS

Since the lids have less density than the water, they float in the water and buoyancy (the upward force the water is exerting on the lids) keeps them on the surface of the water.

VARIATIONS

For younger kids, draw shapes on the lids and have them identify each shape as they draw it out of the water. Letters can also be written on the lids for a fun spelling game. Choose 6 to 7 lids and make words with the letters.

MATERIALS

- Large, shallow baking dish
- Permanent black marker
- Lids in two different colors (any type of plastic lid would work such as milk gallon lids, baby food pouch lids, etc.)
- Paper

DIRECTIONS

Fill the dish with about 1 inch (2.5 cm) of water. Write the numbers 1 through 10 on the tops of one set of same-colored lids. On the other set of lids, write the math symbol you are focusing on such as + or −. Add all the lids to the water facedown so you can't see what's written on each lid.

To play, choose one lid that has a number on it, then one lid that has a math symbol on it, and finally one more lid that has a number on it. Write a math fact on the paper using the numbers and symbol you just drew. Solve the math problem for the math fact you just picked out of the water. Once solved, place the lids back into the water and do it again!

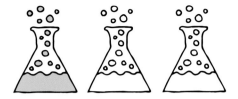

THE "GUESS HOW MANY?" ESTIMATION CHALLENGE

Learning to estimate is an important life skill and is an essential concept as it relates to mathematics. When learning mathematical concepts and techniques, being able to estimate an answer helps you to know if the final calculation is likely correct or not. This activity makes learning to estimate a game, and it's always more fun to learn a skill when it's disguised as a game!

MATERIALS

- 70–200 small household objects such as paper clips, gumballs, rice, water beads, beans, candy, etc., divided
- 1 small, clear container
- 1 large, clear container
- 2 or more players

DIRECTIONS

Place 10 to 20 of one of the small household objects in the small container. Then have an adult (or someone not playing the game) place 50 to 200 in the larger container. The adult should know exactly how many items are in the large container. Inform the participants how many objects are in the small container and ask them to use their estimation skills to guess how many are in the large container. Set up several of these scenarios. See who can guess the closest amount for each object.

VARIATION

Ask your parents for a small amount of money (like $5.00) when going to a dollar store and ask them to allow you to spend it as you want, but without going over the amount. Many items in the store are priced at $1.79 or $2.49. This causes you to have to round up or down and gets you estimating in real life. You will go back and forth adding things and removing them as you find new things and need to keep estimating how much you are spending.

THE HOWS AND WHYS

Learning to estimate is very important in school and in life. For example, when you are shopping and you know you have only $20.00 to spend, you will estimate the cost of each item you put in the cart so as not to go over that amount. In school, learning to estimate gives you a technique for a higher level of understanding when solving math problems. If you can estimate a problem like 19 + 27 by rounding (or estimating) to the nearest 10 (in this case 20 + 30 = 50), you will be able to check your actual answer back to your estimate (in this case 46 is about equal to 50) and know your answer is more likely to be correct.

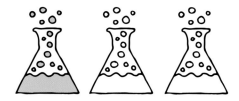

COUNTING IN NATURE

Getting out in nature is always a good idea! Breathing fresh air and moving your body is important to your health. Here's a way to add some math fun to a nature walk.

MATERIALS

◦ Notepad

◦ Pencil

DIRECTIONS

Head outside for a walk with the notepad and pencil. Make a list of 5 items you are going to look for on your nature walk and write the categories in your notepad. Be sure to leave space between the items so you can make tally marks as you spot the items. Some fun things to look for and keep count of are types of flowers, squirrels, rabbits, birds, fire hydrants, etc. Practice making the tally marks nice and straight and making every fifth tally mark a diagonal over the previous four marks. This will help you count your totals faster when the walk is over. Once the walk is over, see if you found the same amount as others. Which item did you find the most of? Which one did you find the least of?

THE HOWS AND WHYS

There are so many things to explore on a nature walk, but I find that giving you something to focus on really heightens your awareness of nature. Sometimes we miss all the beauty right in front of us, but when we are using our sense of sight to try to spot things, we discover lots of other interesting finds along the way.

VARIATIONS

Try counting your steps to get to various places like from the sidewalk to the front door or the number of steps to walk one block. Try collecting interesting nature finds as they are spotted, like pretty leaves, pine cones or wildflowers. Categorize and count your findings when you return home.

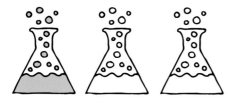

DICE MATH FACTS

Practicing math facts can be a bit ho-hum sometimes, but I find that by adding new elements like dice really spices up practicing these facts and can make learning fun!

MATERIALS

- 2 dice
- Notepad (optional)
- Pencil (optional)

DIRECTIONS

Decide what type of math facts you want to practice: addition, subtraction, multiplication or division. Roll the dice and use the two numbers you rolled to make a math fact. If you want, you can write the math fact down or just do the calculation in your head and shout out the answer. Make it a game with others by seeing who can come up with the correct answer first! Try timing yourself to see how many math facts you can do in 1 minute.

THE HOWS AND WHYS

Many games rely on simple math, and the more you play with numbers, the more likely adding, subtracting, multiplying and dividing become second-nature . . . and fun.

VARIATIONS

Add a third or fourth die and make the math problems more challenging. Or use the two numbers rolled to do all different types of math facts. For example, if you roll a 2 and a 3 you can make the math facts: 2 + 3, 3 + 2, 2 − 3, 3 − 2, 2 x 3, 3 x 2, 2 ÷ 3 and 3 ÷ 2.

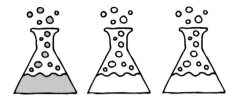

MIRROR GEOMETRIC ART

Here's a fun way to make beautiful geometric art using only two mirrors and any loose items you can find around the house!

THE HOWS AND WHYS

Mirrors are flat surfaces covered in a silver or aluminum layer that reflect light and give us an image of what we look like or what objects we put in front of it look like. When the reflective parts of the mirror face each other at close enough angles, they reflect back onto each other multiple times depending on the angle and give us the illusion of the same object repeating over and over in a geometric pattern.

MATERIALS

- 2 square mirrors or a small compact with 2 mirrors in it that can be stood on its side
- Masking tape
- Small, loose objects such as coins, rocks, straws cut into small pieces and/or toothpicks

DIRECTIONS

Tape the back of the mirrors together so that the reflective sides of the mirror are facing each other at about a 60-degree angle (see photo on page 105). You can make the angle larger or smaller for a different effect. Stand the mirrors up vertically on a table. In the area between the mirrors lay some of your objects down and watch how they reflect within the mirrors in a geometric pattern. Keep adding objects until your creation is complete!

VARIATIONS

Cut out small shapes like squares, circles and triangles with colored construction paper and see what amazing art you can make. Try using small fruits and vegetables like blueberries, carrots and banana slices to make fun and yummy art!

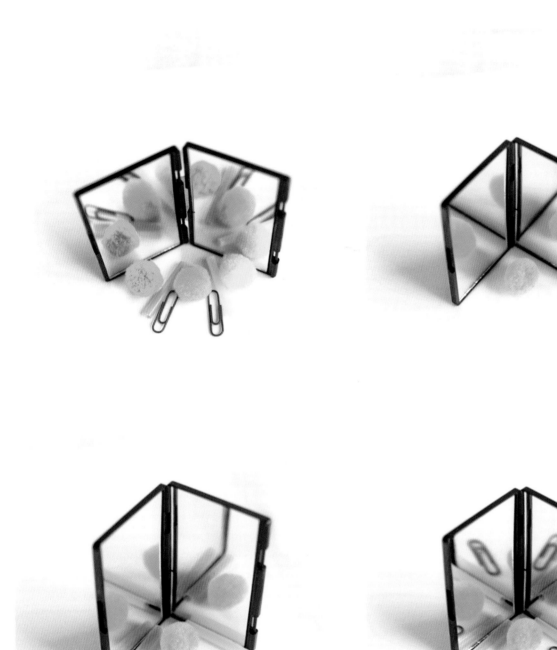

6

TODDLER
STEAM PLAY
IDEAS

It's never too early to be introduced to the concepts of STEAM. Even at age 2, many of us are starting to stack and build and use our amazingly creative minds. At this age, it's important to build core motor skills, so these activities incorporate both STEAM and early development skills. Most of the activities that follow are excellent for kids of any age, but they are appropriate for toddlers as well, so I wanted to group them this way. Activities like Pasta Towers (page 118) or Reverse Drawing (page 127) are super fun for kids of all ages (and even adults)!

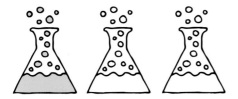

PLAYDOUGH MAZE

Mazes are so much fun to solve *and* build! This awesome activity allows you to show your creativity while building fine motor and oral motor skills.

MATERIALS

- Playdough
- 1 large baking pan or flat surface
- 1 ping pong ball
- Straw

DIRECTIONS

Roll out several long lines of playdough. Shape the playdough lines into a maze on the pan or flat surface. Keep the lines thin, which makes it more challenging to keep the ball in the maze or make them thicker to help keep the ball in the maze. Finally, place a ping pong ball at the start of the maze and use a straw to blow the ping pong ball through the maze.

THE HOWS AND WHYS

Kneading and rolling playdough is great for developing fine motor skills and using the straw to blow the ball is excellent for building oral motor skills.

VARIATION

Roll 1 long piece of playdough and make a long spiral starting in the middle and swirling it bigger and bigger. Leave enough room for the ping pong ball to move between the playdough path of the spiral. Then start the ball on the outside of the spiral and use the straw to move the ball around and around the spiral until it reaches the center.

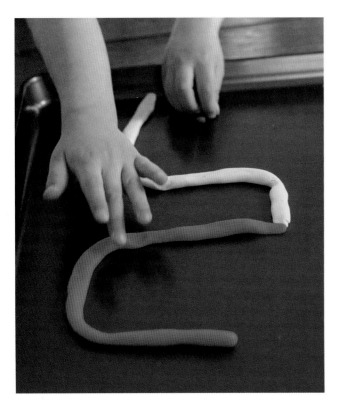

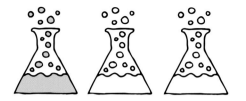

STACKING CUPS

Stacking cups is one of the most basic building activities that's so much fun to do! Here I am modifying it slightly by adding index cards that allow the cups to be turned both upside down and right side up and makes for more interesting and elaborate creations.

MATERIALS
- 50–100 small paper or plastic cups
- 25–50 index cards or cardboard cutouts

DIRECTIONS
Gather your materials and start building! Build a structure such as a wall or a fort using both materials. For more challenges, build the tallest tower you can, a bridge or certain shapes like a rectangle, triangle or square.

THE HOWS AND WHYS
The cups and cutouts are easy to work with and allow you to build structures and use your creativity to come up with amazing creations. This activity is great for concentration, patience and fine motor skills as well.

VARIATION
Build a bridge with the cups and cards and add little toys or coins to see how much weight the bridge can hold.

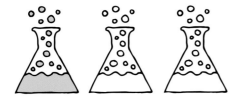

STICKY NOTE MYSTERY BOX

Sticky notes make great wrapping paper, and working with sticky notes is an excellent fine motor activity! Use any clear container you have around the house to complete this fun activity.

THE HOWS AND WHYS

Adding and removing the sticky notes requires lots of movement with your fingers and builds fine motor skills. The notes can also get stuck to your hands, which gives you an extra challenge. This activity will also spark your curiosity as you start to uncover the container and try to see what is inside. It's a fun discovery activity!

VARIATION

Have a friend or parent create patterns with the sticky notes on a table or wall and see if you can replicate the patterns.

MATERIALS

- 2 players
- Clear resealable container like a plastic pickle jar
- Items to fill the container with such as rice (which makes a sound when shaken), small dinosaur toys, food bits or animal crackers
- Sticky notes (the more colors the better)
- Scissors (optional)
- 1 pencil (optional)

DIRECTIONS

Have one player fill the container with some fun objects that will be uncovered as the sticky notes are removed during the activity. If you include rice, the mystery container will make a fun noise when you shake it! Then have them seal the container and add the sticky notes to the outside to completely cover the container. You can cut up the sticky notes with a pair of scissors to make smaller pieces or try curling the ends up using a pencil. Once the container is completely covered up, have the other player remove all the sticky notes and discover what's underneath! Once all the notes are removed, you can twist and turn the container to see all the fun surprises inside. Once you are done looking inside the container, you can "wrap" the package back up with the sticky notes. Empty the container and have the present opener become the present creator!

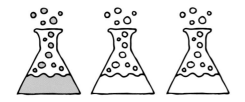

PASTA TOWERS

Want to take your playdough creations to the next level? Toss in some pasta and get ready for some amazing creations!

MATERIALS

° Playdough (1 or many colors)

° Uncooked pasta (Any kind will work but my favorites are penne, rigatoni, linguini and spaghetti.)

DIRECTIONS

Roll the playdough into balls and insert pieces of the uncooked pasta into them. Keep adding pasta and playdough to build a structure such as a tower. Challenge each other to make the tallest tower possible, either by working together or as a competition. This is especially fun if you have linguini or spaghetti.

THE HOWS AND WHYS

The pasta sticks well to the playdough and allows the creations to go vertical, making it easier to build towers and taller structures.

VARIATION

Use pasta and playdough to make an animal! Add some googly eyes to make the creatures come alive even more.

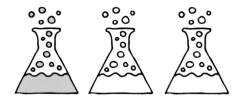

SINK OR FLOAT

Here's a fun activity to learn about the concepts of buoyancy and density by testing whether common household objects sink or float in water.

THE HOWS AND WHYS

Density is a measure of the amount of space something takes up in relation to the amount of matter it has. If something is very heavy but small (like a rock) it has a high density, but if something is large and light (like a foam block) it has a low density. This experiment tests if objects have a higher or lower density than water. If the object sinks in water it has a higher density than water, and if it floats, it has a lower density than water. If an object has a lower density than water, we can say it has buoyancy, which is the ability to float in water.

MATERIALS

- 1 towel
- 1 bucket or basin
- Water
- Household objects such as lids, coins, small toys, a pencil, keys, kitchen utensils, building block toys, crayons, a ball of foil, grapes, blueberries and/or an orange
- Paper and pencil

DIRECTIONS

Place a towel on the ground or on a table. I like doing this activity outdoors if it's nice, but if you're indoors, you will definitely want a towel to absorb any spills and a place to place the objects once they come out of the water. Fill the bucket about halfway full of water and then select an object to drop in the water. Make a prediction if you think the object will sink or float. After you make a prediction, drop the item in the water and see if you were right. Make a list with two columns labeled "Sink" and "Float" and draw pictures of the objects in the right column after you test each one.

VARIATIONS

Do this activity in the bathtub to make bath time even more fun and educational! Another fun variation is adding a few drops of food coloring to the water to give it some color!

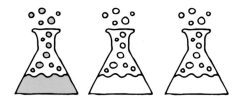

CRAFT STICK PUZZLE

This craft stick puzzle is so simple to make and it's helpful for learning colors, shapes, letters or numbers based on what you are trying to learn.

MATERIALS

- 8 craft sticks, not colored
- Tape
- Markers

DIRECTIONS

Line up the craft sticks side by side and flat (see photo). Apply 2 rows of tape across the sticks to hold them in place. Flip the craft sticks over so the taped side is on the bottom. Draw a puzzle design across all of the craft sticks. Focus your design on a concept like colors, shapes, letters or numbers. Once the drawing is complete, remove the tape from the other side. Jumble up the pieces so they are out of order and then put them back in the correct order to solve the puzzle.

THE HOWS AND WHYS

Puzzles are a great first step in early engineering concepts as they require problem solving, patience and 2-D building skills. You learn to focus on a task and are rewarded with a beautiful picture at the end of your work. It is also great for building fine motor skills as you move the pieces around trying to solve the puzzle.

VARIATION

Have a friend create their own puzzle by doing the drawing themselves on the craft sticks and then try to solve their puzzle.

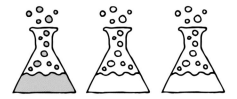

CEREAL BOX PUZZLE

Cereal boxes are so bright and colorful with great combinations of words and pictures that they make great templates for a DIY puzzle. And the best part is that the back of the puzzle is blank and can be drawn on to make your own design as well for a two-sided puzzle experience.

MATERIALS

- Scissors
- 1 empty cereal box
- Markers or crayons (optional)
- Resealable plastic bag (for storage)

DIRECTIONS

Cut out the front panel of the cereal box so you have a large rectangle. If you would like to make a double-sided puzzle, turn the rectangle face down to reveal the blank side and create a drawing on the blank side using markers or crayons. Once the drawing is complete, cut the cardboard into puzzle pieces. Make some with straight edges and some with wavy edges. You can make small or large pieces depending on how difficult you want the puzzle to be. Once the sheet is cut into pieces, mix them up, lay them all out and then solve the puzzle.

THE HOWS AND WHYS

Puzzles are great for 2-D building and problem solving. They are also great for learning focus, concentration and patience since it takes time to solve the puzzles. You need to look for patterns and try to align the pieces to complete the picture. The blank side of the sheet allows you to express your creativity and create your own version of a puzzle to solve.

VARIATION

Create 2 puzzles using 2 different cereal boxes and mix them together for an additional challenge.

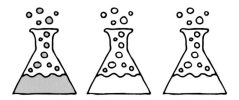

BEND THE WATER

Static electricity occurs when electrical charges build up on the surfaces of objects. It can cause crazy things to happen, like when your hair sticks straight up from your head or when you touch your friend and give them a little zap. In this experiment you will actually cause water to bend as it flows from a faucet using static electricity.

VARIATIONS

Test different temperatures of water to see if the bend changes. Test a large stream of water versus a small stream. Try the experiment using a comb instead of a balloon.

MATERIALS

◦ 1 latex balloon
◦ Faucet with running water

DIRECTIONS

Inflate the balloon. Turn on the faucet so that a small stream of cool water flows. Hold the balloon next to the faucet and notice if the water changes direction (it shouldn't). Now rub the balloon against your hair for about 10 seconds. Place the balloon next to the running water and watch what happens. The stream of water actually bends toward the balloon!

THE HOWS AND WHYS

Atoms are made up of neutrons, protons and electrons. In a normal state, most items maintain a neutral charge, but when the balloon is rubbed against your head, electrons are transferred to the balloon, giving it a negative charge. When the negatively charged balloon is held near the water (which has a slightly positive charge), the opposite charges are attracted to each other and the water bends toward the balloon. You may also have noticed your hair sticking up after you rubbed the balloon on it. This is because your hair now has a positive charge since some of the electrons were transferred to the balloon. Since the hairs are positively charged, they repel each other and try to separate causing them to stick up.

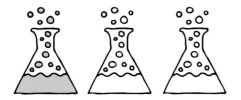

SHAVING CREAM COLOR MIXING

Shaving cream has such a fun sensory feel, but it can be a bit messy to play with. This activity introduces a mess-free way to experiment with color mixing while enjoying the tactile qualities of shaving cream.

THE HOWS AND WHYS

There are three primary colors: red, yellow and blue. When two of these colors are mixed, they form secondary colors: red + yellow = orange, yellow + blue = green and red + blue = purple. The shaving cream absorbs the color you added, but it takes work to get the colors to mix, and you have to move the shaving cream around quite a bit to get the colors to blend. This is because shaving cream is classified as a foam, which is a liquid (soap and water) mixed with tiny gas bubbles, giving it unique properties and making for fun sensory play.

MATERIALS

• 1-gallon (3.8-L) resealable plastic bag
• Shaving cream
• Red, blue and yellow liquid food coloring
• Packing or painter's tape

DIRECTIONS

Lay the bag on a table, flat on one side, and spray the shaving cream into the bag so it rests on the side touching the table. It makes it easier to add the color if the top of the bag is not touching the shaving cream yet. Add 6 to 8 drops of each color of food coloring to different sections of the shaving cream. By keeping the colors separate it allows you to move the shaving cream around to mix the colors. Press the bag flat to remove as much air as possible and seal the bag. Apply tape to the top and bottom of the bag to secure it to the table. Now mix the colors by pressing on the shaving cream and moving it around the bag. Can you predict what will happen when red and yellow mix? Blue and red? Blue and yellow?

VARIATION

Use the shaving cream bag to trace shapes, letters or numbers for additional sensory learning.

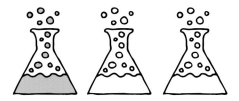

REVERSE DRAWING

We typically think of creating a drawing by adding lines or colors to a blank canvas, but this activity takes this idea and turns it upside down.

MATERIALS

- Pencil or erasable crayons
- White paper
- Eraser

DIRECTIONS

Shade in the paper completely with the pencil or a dark color erasable crayon. Darker is better in terms of how heavy to fill it in. If it's too light, you will not be able to see the reverse drawing come through as much in the end. Use the eraser to "draw" your design by erasing the pencil or crayon. Keep erasing until your drawing is complete!

THE HOWS AND WHYS

Shading in a whole piece of paper takes patience and concentration. It is also great for practicing holding a pencil and building fine motor skills. Then creating art using the eraser requires a change in our thinking to understand that the eraser is now the drawing utensil, and that we will be creating our art by removing color rather than adding it. Challenging our normal way of thinking helps you learn to think outside the box and builds creativity when learning to solve problems.

VARIATIONS

Try shading in the paper with heavy lines versus lighter lines. Use different-sized erasers to make different types of pictures.

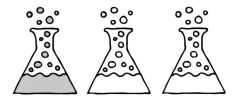

IS IT MAGNETIC?

Magnetism is one of the first scientific concepts we are introduced to. Many kids' toys have a magnetic component and the magical mystery captivates us from an early age. Here is a fun activity to teach you about magnetism in everyday objects.

THE HOWS AND WHYS

Magnetism is a physics concept in which forces either attract or repel objects that have certain properties. Magnets produce a magnetic field, which causes objects made of iron, nickel or cobalt to be attracted to it. Each magnet has two poles, a north pole and a south pole. Opposite poles of magnets attract (pull towards) each other and similar poles repel (push away) each other.

MATERIALS

- Magnetic household items such as paper clips, tweezers, scouring sponges, food cans, sewing needles, tools, key rings, nuts and bolts, staples and/or batteries
- Non-magnetic household items such as pencils, crayons, plastic cups, toys, building blocks
- Magnet

DIRECTIONS

Gather the common household items, some of which are magnetic, some of which are not and some that you're not sure of. Pick up an item and make a prediction: is it magnetic or not? How can you tell? Why do you think it might be magnetic? Check to see if your prediction is correct by placing the magnet on the object. If it sticks, it's magnetic! Place the item in a pile for magnetic or non-magnetic objects. Continue to test all the items you collected, and in the end, you will have two piles with magnetic and non-magnetic items. Once you've tested all the items, take a look at both piles and see if you can come up with any conclusions about why some items are magnetic. What do all the magnetic items have in common? How are they different?

VARIATION

Drop a paper clip in a glass vase filled with water and use the magnet to try and get the paper clip out of the vase by lifting the paper clip with the magnet through the wall of the vase.

7

SEASONAL STEAM ACTIVITIES

Getting into the season is fun! And as the seasons change, it's also nice to change up the activities and have some go-to ideas that are seasonal or holiday-themed. In the spring and summer, I like to move the activities outside as much as possible! This also allows us to get a bit messier! In the fall and winter, I like to use themes like leaves, pumpkins and snow for the activities.

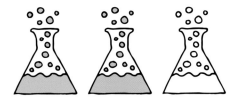

RAISED-SALT PAINTING

Spring is such a beautiful time of year when trees bud and flowers bloom. It's a perfect time to use a technique called raised-salt painting to create beautiful flowers!

THE HOWS AND WHYS

The glue and salt create a raised, textured surface that keeps the color from spreading on the paper to create brightly colored, beautiful lines. This allows the colors to blend and spread beautifully within the salt lines.

MATERIALS

- 1 pencil
- White paper or cardstock (thicker paper works better)
- Baking sheet or tray
- White glue in a squeeze bottle
- Salt
- 2 or more small cups or containers to hold watercolors
- Water
- Liquid food coloring
- Pipettes or paintbrushes

DIRECTIONS

Lightly sketch your flower on the white paper with the pencil. Place the paper on the baking sheet and trace over your design with the white glue. Sprinkle salt over all the glue. Once all the glue is thoroughly covered with salt, carefully pick the paper up and gently shake off all the excess salt onto the tray or directly into the trash.

Fill the cups with a little bit of water. Use just a little water if you want your colors to be more concentrated. Add 4 to 5 drops of food coloring to the cups. Make as many colors as you want. Use the pipette to apply small amounts of color directly on the salt in the painting. The salt absorbs the color beautifully and blends well with other colors as they are applied. Once all the color has been applied to the salt, allow the painting to sit flat to dry completely for a day or so.

VARIATIONS

Try using black paper and make fireworks for the 4th of July or New Year's Eve! This activity can work well for any holiday: hearts for Valentine's Day, shamrocks and rainbows for St. Patrick's Day or pumpkins and ghosts for Halloween. Another fun technique is to create a regular watercolor painting and sprinkle salt onto the painting while it's still wet. The salt will absorb the watercolor pigments, creating a fun effect on the painting.

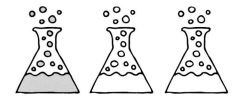

STANDING EGG EXPERIMENT

If you've ever studied an egg, you know that they are oval shaped and have no flat side. Have you ever tried getting an egg to stand upright? It seems impossible, but in this experiment, we'll do just that using just a sprinkle of salt!

MATERIALS
- Raw egg (in the shell)
- A pinch of table salt

DIRECTIONS

Try to make the egg stand up straight on a flat surface. What happens? As soon as you let go of the egg, it falls to its side. Place a pinch of salt on the table and place the egg right in the middle of the salt and see if you can get it to stand up straight. It may take a couple tries but the egg should stay standing when you take your hands away. Once the egg is standing, blow away the excess salt and the egg will appear to be magically standing on its end.

THE HOWS AND WHYS

Tiny salt crystals are almost perfect cubes. These tiny cubes work like a pedestal to stabilize and support the egg and keep it standing upright.

VARIATIONS

Make it a competition and see who can balance an egg on its end in the shortest amount of time. Try blowing on the egg to see how much force it takes to knock the egg down.

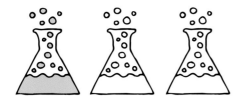

WALKING PAPER WHEEL

Here's a great teamwork activity that can be done indoors or outdoors, so it's perfect for spring. You are going to make a large wheel with just a long piece of butcher paper or the packing paper that comes in shipments and some tape.

THE HOWS AND WHYS

This activity requires patience and teamwork to make the wheel function. You must work together to take coordinated steps or the wheel will not function properly. It also requires some thought to construct the wheel correctly.

MATERIALS

° 1 piece of butcher paper or packing paper (about 15 x 2 feet [4.5 x 0.6 m] wide)
° Packing tape
° Paints, markers or crayons (optional)
° Lots of friends

DIRECTIONS

Lay the paper flat on the ground. Tape the long ends of the paper together, creating a giant circle or wheel that you and a few friends can fit inside. You can decorate the outside of the wheel to personalize it in whatever way you want or leave it plain. With your feet on the bottom of the wheel and your hands over your head touching the top of the wheel, stand in a line with your friends and take small steps forward, which causes the paper wheel to move forward as well. This takes practice and teamwork as you move together . . . otherwise the paper will rip and need to be repaired.

VARIATION

If you have enough people, create two wheels and have them race. The first team to pass the finish line without breaking the wheel wins.

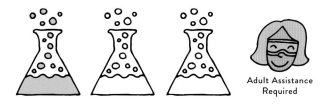

BUBBLE SNAKES

Bubbles are one of those things that are fun to make, chase, play with and learn about. Here you are going to make long chains of bubbles called bubble snakes with a simple bubble blower you can make yourself! This is definitely an outdoor activity!

MATERIALS

- Scissors
- 1 empty water bottle
- 1 sock
- 1 rubber band
- 1 tbsp (15 ml) dish soap
- ½ cup (120 ml) water
- 1 bowl

DIRECTIONS

Have an adult help cut the bottom off the end of the empty water bottle. Fit the sock over the end of the water bottle with the missing bottom. Place a rubber band around the sock to secure it onto the water bottle. Prepare your bubble mix by adding the dish soap and water to the bowl and mixing. Dip the sock-covered end of the water bottle into the bubble mix. Once the end is fully soaked, lift it up and blow through the drinking end of the bottle. Watch as a bubble snake emerges from the end of the bottle! Try blowing slowly and gently into the bottle. Notice how the bubbles are bigger and you can see through the bubble snake. Now try blowing faster and harder into the bottle. Notice the bubbles are smaller and you can't see through the bubble snake. Note: Be sure not to inhale or you will breathe in the bubbles.

THE HOWS AND WHYS

When you blew softly and gently through the bottle, could you see through the bubble snake? This is because the bubbles were bigger. When we can see through an object, we say the object is transparent. Transparency is when an object allows light to pass through it and see what is on the other side. What other objects can you name that are transparent? When you blew faster and harder on the bottle, the bubbles were smaller and you could not see through the bubble snake as well. In this case, we would say the bubble snake is translucent. Something is translucent when you can't see through an object but light is still allowed to pass through. What other objects can you name that are translucent?

VARIATION

Add liquid food coloring to the sock at the opening of the bottle. Then dip in the bubble mix and blow to get colored bubble snakes!

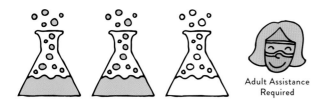

Adult Assistance
Required

POOL NOODLE OBSTACLE COURSE

What is better than an obstacle course in the summer? Well this one is so simple to set up and will have you running around outdoors for hours!

MATERIALS

- 15 or more pool noodles in various colors
- 18 or more sharpened pencils, wooden dowels or tent stakes
- Duct tape
- Bread knife (for adult use only)

DIRECTIONS

This course has 5 different stations.

1. Tunnels: To create the tunnels, place 2 pencils about 2 to 3 feet (61 to 91 cm) apart by sticking the sharp end of the pencil in the ground. Place the ends of 1 pool noodle over the pencils to create an arch. Repeat this step 2 more times. Older kids could use these as hurdles. These tunnels are really fun, so you may want to make more like we did! (See photo.)

2. Mini-hurdles: To create these hurdles, take a full-length pool noodle and stick the sharp end of a pencil into the noodle about 1 foot (30 cm) from the end on each side. Once you make a hole, remove the pencil and place the eraser end into the pool noodle. Repeat for each side and then with the sharp ends of the pencils sticking out of the noodles, stick them into the ground. Repeat 2 more times to make 3 hurdles.

4. Balance beam: To create a balance beam, place a noodle flat on the grass and secure it into the ground on each end by sticking the sharp end of a pencil through the inner part of the noodle and into the ground. Be sure the pencil is pushed all the way though the noodle so it is deep into the ground and no pencil is sticking up. Another option is to use tent stakes for this portion.

5. In and out: Add 3 or 4 vertical noodles that you can weave in and out of to finish the course. To create these, stick pencils in the ground in a line about 3 to 4 feet (91 to 122 cm) apart. Add 1 noodle to each pencil sticking up and that's it!

Finally, to create a finish line, lay 1 noodle flat at the end of the course.

3. Ring toss: Take 2 pool noodles and loop each of them into circles until the ends touch. With the ends touching flat against each other, wrap them in duct tape several times around so the rings don't come apart. Have an adult cut another noodle in half with the bread knife, then stick a pencil in the ground and place one of the half noodles over the pencil. Use the other half noodle as a line to stand behind when doing the ring toss.

THE HOWS AND WHYS

This course is simple to construct and you don't even need parents to help you build it, which makes it a great engineering activity!

VARIATIONS

What other obstacles can you come up with using just pool noodles, duct tape and pencils? Use your imagination! Time the racers to see who can finish the course the fastest or do team relays!

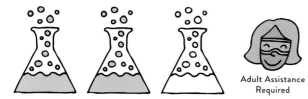

Adult Assistance Required

POOL NOODLE AND SHAVING CREAM BUILDING

Pool noodles can make great building blocks! In this messy activity you will cut the noodles into a variety of shapes and use shaving cream as your "glue" to build all kinds of structures. This is definitely an outdoor activity as it can get messy, but it's guaranteed to be fun!

MATERIALS

- 2 pool noodles
- Bread knife (for adult use only)
- Shaving cream
- 1 bowl
- Kid's knife (optional)

DIRECTIONS

Have an adult cut up the pool noodles with the bread knife. Make all kinds of shapes including cylinders of all sizes, semicircles, quarter circles and straight pieces. The more shapes the better. Place some shaving cream in the bowl. Build your structures using the shaving cream to hold the pieces of pool noodle together like glue. You can use a kid's knife (or plastic knife) to help spread the shaving cream onto the pieces or you can use your fingers, a stick or just dip the pool noodle pieces into the bowl. Try different techniques to see what works best. What types of things can you create? Animals, buildings, towers?

THE HOWS AND WHYS

Shaving cream is a great sensory material, and it's just fun to play with and get messy. It also works well to hold the pool noodle pieces together. The pool noodles are very light and allow for lots of different 3-D ideas to come to life, making for an excellent building and design activity.

VARIATIONS

Try building the tallest tower possible using the pool noodles and shaving cream. Try building with pool noodle pieces without the shaving cream. Is it more difficult?

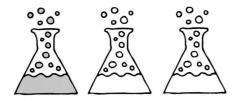

STANDING POOL NOODLE GAME

Pool noodles are one of my favorite materials to use in games, art projects and building activities! They are just so versatile. Here is a fun way to use the noodles for a game that teaches you about balance and speed.

MATERIALS

° As many players as you can find
° 1 pool noodle for each player

DIRECTIONS

Start the game with everyone standing in a circle a few feet apart while holding their pool noodles straight up. Have someone yell, "1, 2, 3, Go!" at which point all the players let go of their noodle and move in a clockwise direction to the next noodle. The goal is to keep the noodles from hitting the ground for as many rounds as possible. After 5 to 6 rounds, have everyone take a step out to make it a little more challenging. If a noodle falls, the person that failed to catch it is out. See how many rounds the group can go before only 1 person is left.

THE HOWS AND WHYS

This game requires teamwork, balance and speed. Your group is trying to coordinate their movements using the "1, 2, 3, GO!" command so you all move at the same time. You also need to keep your noodle balanced upright so the next person can catch your noodle before it falls to the ground. If the noodle is not balanced well, it will fall before the next person can reach it. You also need to use speed to quickly get from one noodle to the next. If you move too slowly, the noodle will fall to the ground.

VARIATIONS

Make the game an individual challenge to see who can last the longest without dropping a noodle. Try using large sticks, baseball bats or lacrosse sticks instead of pool noodles.

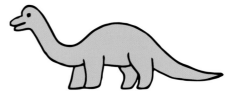

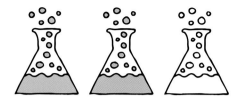

WATER BALLOON PAINTING

Is there anything more fun than playing with water balloons in the summer? We all know how much fun it is to throw them around, but did you know you can make beautiful artwork with them as well?

THE HOWS AND WHYS

Water balloon painting is an excellent process art activity. Process art is when the focus is on the creative process and not on the end product. Balloons are an unconventional tool to use to create art, and allows you to think differently and creatively about how you can use the balloons to make art.

MATERIALS

- Water balloons
- Water
- 1 large roll of easel paper or butcher paper
- 4 large rocks
- Washable tempera paints
- Containers to hold the paint (big enough to dip the water balloons into them)

DIRECTIONS

Fill up a few balloons with water. Try not to fill them too full as you don't want them to burst while painting with them. (Although the chance that they may burst makes it all the more fun!) Lay the paper down on the ground and secure the corners with rocks so the wind doesn't blow the paper away. Add your paint to the containers. Dip a balloon in some paint and start painting on the paper. There are lots of different ways to use the balloons. Try rolling, spinning, dabbing and swirling them in loops to make beautiful patterns on the paper. Allow the artwork to completely dry before moving it.

VARIATION

What fun techniques can you come up with using the balloons as paintbrushes? Try filling regular balloons with a small amount of colored water and then poking a small hole in the end using a safety pin. Squeeze the balloon so the colored water starts to come out and see what beautiful splatter painting creations you can make!

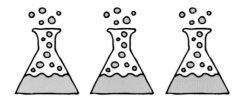

GIANT BUBBLES

Blowing bubbles is a favorite pastime for many, and I love trying to see who can make the biggest bubble. Here's a simple technique to make giant bubbles! This is definitely an outdoors only activity!

THE HOWS AND WHYS

You may have noticed when you are inflating the bubble with air it makes all kinds of funny shapes, but once the bubble is sealed it becomes an almost perfect sphere. This is because once the bubble is sealed the bubble skin has tension and shrinks to the smallest possible shape, which happens to be a sphere.

VARIATIONS

Try bending a hanger (or large wire) into a circular shape and using it as a bubble wand. Try blowing bubbles outside on a cold day. They should rise because the air inside the bubbles will be much warmer than the air outside.

MATERIALS

- Dish soap
- Water
- Large bowl
- Large baking sheet
- 2 plastic straws (about 6 inches [15 cm], with bendy ends cut off)
- 30-inch (76-cm) piece of cotton string

DIRECTIONS

To make your bubble mix, add 1 part dish soap to about 6 parts water to the large bowl. Mix well. Pour the mixture onto a baking sheet. It will be hard to move the baking sheet with the bubble mix in it, so place it strategically before adding the bubble mix.

To make your bubble blower, lace the straws onto the string. Tie the ends of the string together to create a giant loop and move the string until the knot is hidden inside one of the straws. Separate the straws so one is on each side. When you are holding the straws vertically and parallel, your string should make a rectangle.

Dip your bubble blower into the bubble mix and hold it up with the straws close together and the string hanging. This activity works best if there is only a slight wind. Once you hold the bubble blower up, pull the straws apart so the strings are taut. Now either blow into the bubble blower or allow the wind to help you create a giant bubble. The bubble will either naturally separate from the bubble blower and float away or make a gigantic bubble that looks like a big worm.

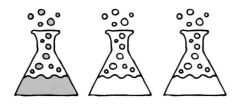

CANDY CORN STACKING CHALLENGE

Candy corns are a staple of the fall season. These delicious little candy kernels are not only fun to eat, but you can actually build them into the shape of a corncob!

MATERIALS

- Bag of candy corn
- 1 paper plate or other nonstick surface

DIRECTIONS

Place a few handfuls of candy corn on the paper plate. Start arranging the candy corns in a circle with the points facing the center of the circle. There should be anywhere from 10 to 15 pieces of candy corn in your base layer circle. Once you've completed the bottom layer, start adding candy corn in a second layer. Place each new piece evenly between 2 pieces on the bottom layer. See how many layers you can build before the corncob tower falls down.

THE HOWS AND WHYS

Candy corns are triangular shaped and wider along the outside of the candy corn and thinner at the center point. This shape allows for the candy to form a circle. The difference in the width from the outside to the inner point will eventually cause the corncob tower you build to fall inward, but it's fun to see how many rows you can build before it tumbles down.

VARIATION

Use a giant marshmallow to push the points of the candy corn into as you are building your corncob. Does this help make the corncob taller?

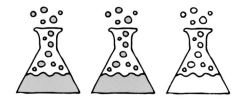

MONSTER SLIME

Why do we love slime so much? Maybe it's the texture or the fact that we mix a few ingredients that aren't slime-like at all and we end up with stretchy, squishy goodness. Who knows, but here's a fun Halloween twist on my favorite slime recipe.

THE HOWS AND WHYS

Slime is both a polymer and a non-Newtonian fluid. Non-Newtonian fluids behave differently than normal fluids such as water. If you pull it slowly it stretches into long strings, but if you pull it apart quickly, it will break apart as the chemical bonds are broken. Slime is also a polymer. Polymers are made up of lots of small molecules that form long, flexible chains. When a slime activator like contact solution is added to a polymer like glue, a process called cross linking occurs and causes the long chains of molecules in the glue to become all tangled up and less viscose. This is how slime is formed!

MATERIALS

- ½ cup (120 ml) clear school glue
- ½ tsp baking soda
- Liquid food coloring
- 1 spoon or spatula to mix (I prefer a disposable spoon.)
- 1 bowl
- 1–2 tbsp (15–30 ml) contact lens solution
- Vegetable or baby oil (optional but can help with sticking)
- Googly eyes with nonstick backs
- Plastic vampire fangs
- Resealable plastic bags

DIRECTIONS

In the bowl mix together the glue, baking soda and a few drops of food coloring. (Using clear glue allows the monsters to be slightly transparent and extra creepy!) When fully mixed, add 1 tablespoon (15 ml) of the contact solution and mix. Keep adding contact solution until the slime stops sticking to the bowl and can be picked up without sticking to your hands. If you find the slime still sticking to your hands, add a few drops of oil (any kind will work) and this will help keep the slime from sticking. Finally, add some googly eyes and vampire fangs and start creating your monsters! If your slime starts to get too solid or dry out, add a bit of water and knead it into the slime to get it stretchy again. Be sure to store your slime in resealable plastic bags to keep it from drying out.

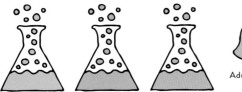

Adult Assistance
Required

ERUPTING PUMPKINS

Carving pumpkins is something I look forward to every year! But once I tried these erupting pumpkins, it no longer became about carving . . . it's all about the erupting pumpkins!

THE HOWS AND WHYS

The chemical reaction when baking soda and vinegar are mixed is an acid-base reaction. Vinegar is an acid and baking soda is a base. When they are mixed, one of the products produced is a gas called carbon dioxide. This is what causes the fizzing and bubbling eruption flowing out of the pumpkin.

MATERIALS

- 1 small baking pumpkin (You can use larger pumpkins, but you will need a lot of vinegar and baking soda.)
- Baking sheet or large baking pan
- Carving knife (for adult use only)
- Spoon or scooper
- 1 heaping tbsp (14 g) baking soda, or more
- Dish soap
- Liquid food coloring (optional)
- 1 cup (240 ml) white vinegar, or more

DIRECTIONS

Place the pumpkin on a baking sheet or in a large baking pan. Have an adult cut a small hole in the top of the pumpkin around the stem. Remove the stem and then the seeds and pumpkin meat inside the pumpkin using a spoon or scooper. Add the baking soda, a big squirt of dish soap and a few drops of food coloring to the pumpkin. Finally, pour in the vinegar and watch the pumpkin erupt! Depending on the size of the pumpkin, you may need to add more baking soda and/or vinegar. Just keep adding until the bubbly eruption happens.

VARIATION

Have an adult help you cut a face into a larger pumpkin to make a jack-o'-lantern before adding the vinegar. If you do this, you will need to use a Mason jar inside your pumpkin to mix the baking soda and vinegar. Once the lava starts flowing, it will come out of the mouth, nose and eyes!

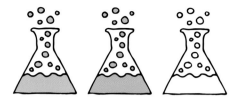

BALLOON MONSTERS

Monsters are so fun to draw, and in this activity you are going to draw monsters that grow bigger and bigger!

THE HOWS AND WHYS

The chemical reaction when baking soda and vinegar are mixed is an acid-base reaction. Vinegar is an acid and baking soda is a base. When they are mixed, one of the products produced is a gas called carbon dioxide. As the gas tries to escape the bottle, the balloon inflates.

MATERIALS

- Latex balloons
- Permanent markers
- 1 cup (240 ml) white vinegar
- 1 empty water bottle
- 1 tsp baking soda, or more if needed
- 1 funnel

DIRECTIONS

Draw a monster on a latex balloon with the permanent markers. Pour the vinegar into the water bottle. Pour the baking soda into the balloon with the funnel. Cover the opening of the water bottle with the open end of the balloon. Allow the baking soda in the balloon to fall into the vinegar and watch what happens! The balloon inflates and your monster grows bigger and bigger!

VARIATIONS

Try using an ink pad to place a fingerprint on a balloon and then inflate the balloon using the method above, and you will be able to see an enlarged version of your fingerprint. Notice all the tiny lines that make up your unique fingerprint. Try adjusting the amounts of vinegar and baking soda used to see if the balloon inflates more or less.

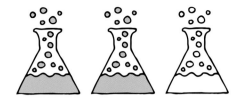

CRAYON RESIST LEAF PRINTS

Fall is that wonderful time of year when the leaves change color and fall from the trees. Here's a fun variation on classic leaf imprints.

THE HOWS AND WHYS

Crayons are made of wax and the wax on the paper resists the watercolor paint and keeps it from coloring the paper. Because white crayon is used, the leaf print cannot be seen until watercolor paint is applied and then the print almost magically appears.

VARIATIONS

Try using other colors of crayons to make leaf prints. Try writing secret messages in white crayon and then revealing those messages with watercolor paint.

MATERIALS

- Leaves of various shapes and sizes
- 1 white crayon
- White watercolor paper (Regular paper will work as well.)
- Tape
- Paintbrush
- Water
- Watercolor paints

DIRECTIONS

Head outside and gather all types of leaves from the ground and trees. Leaves with thicker stems and veins work the best. Peel the paper wrapping off the outside of the white crayon. Place one or more of the leaves under a piece of paper. Tape the top of the paper to the table with 2 pieces of tape. Take the white crayon and rub it on top of the paper with the long side of the crayon on the paper. Focus on doing one leaf rubbing at a time to make sure you get enough white crayon on each leaf. When you are done, wet the paintbrush with some water and apply watercolor paints to the paper. You will start to see the leaf print appear in white as the areas with white crayon will resist the watercolor and beautiful leaf prints will be revealed!

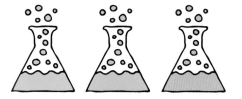

SNOW VOLCANO

When it snows, my kids and I can't wait to get outside and play. This snow volcano has now become a must-do whenever we get a large amount of snow, and it's a great way to incorporate some science into all the fun, snowy play.

THE HOWS AND WHYS

The chemical reaction when baking soda and vinegar are mixed is an acid-base reaction. Vinegar is an acid and baking soda is a base. When they are mixed, one of the products produced is a gas called carbon dioxide. This is what causes all the fizzing and bubbling and what appears to be lava flowing out of the volcano.

MATERIALS

- A big pile of snow
- 1 small plastic bowl
- Vinegar
- Dish soap
- Liquid food coloring
- Baking soda
- 1 spoon

DIRECTIONS

Create a volcano shape out of the big pile of snow. Carve out a shallow hole in the top and place the small plastic bowl in the hole. Fill the bowl with vinegar, a big squirt of dish soap and some food coloring (or liquid watercolors). Add 2 to 3 heaping tablespoons (28 to 41 g) of baking soda, mix with the vinegar and watch the "lava" flow! If the lava isn't flowing, add some more baking soda and/or vinegar until it starts to flow. You can keep changing the colors of your volcano by mixing different colors with vinegar and then adding it to the bowl. When the lava stops flowing, add another tablespoon (14 g) of baking soda and it will start flowing again!

VARIATION

If you live in warm climates that don't get snow, try making a volcano out of sand, dirt and/or rocks. The great thing about doing this activity outside is that there is much less mess to clean up!

WATERCOLOR SNOWFLAKES

Coffee filters make great blank canvases for creating simple art projects. Here you are going to use them to make colorful snowflakes!

MATERIALS

- Red, yellow and blue liquid food coloring
- Small containers to hold the watercolors
- Water
- White coffee filters
- Scissors
- Shallow tray or plate
- 1 dropper or pipette

DIRECTIONS

To make the liquid watercolors, add 3 to 4 drops of food coloring to each small container along with about 1 tablespoon (15 ml) of water. We like making red, yellow and blue watercolors because when they start to mix with each other on the snowflake canvas, new colors are formed.

To make your coffee filter snowflake, fold a filter in half 4 times. You should now have a skinny triangle. Make cuts into the triangle, but be sure not to cut all the way through the triangle or the snowflake will not form. Try cutting triangles, semicircles and squares into the sides of the triangle. Once you've made all your cuts, you are ready to add color. Place the folded-up coffee filter on the tray and take the dropper or pipette and add a few drops of the food coloring paint to the folded-up coffee filter. A few drops go a long way, so add them slowly. Then add some drops of another color. Allow some space in between the colors as they will spread and blend together. Once the coffee filter is fully absorbed with color, you can carefully unfold it to reveal a beautiful, symmetrical snowflake!

VARIATIONS

If you don't want to make watercolors, try using washable markers. Draw on the folded-up snowflakes using the markers only on the top layer, then apply just enough water so that it fully wets the coffee filter. Allow the colors to bleed together to get the same effect.

THE HOWS AND WHYS

When colored water is added to the coffee filter, a process called absorption takes place. Absorption is defined as the process of one thing becoming part of another thing. In this case, the water becomes part of the coffee filter when it is absorbed into the coffee filter. The end result applies colors to the filter and then the water dries up and leaves the color on the filter. This activity is also a great example of color mixing. Red, yellow and blue are primary colors, which means you can't mix other colors to make them. When any two primary colors are mixed, they combine to make secondary colors like orange (red + yellow), green (yellow + blue) or purple (red + blue). Look on the snowflake to see if you can spot these secondary colors at the points where the primary colors meet.

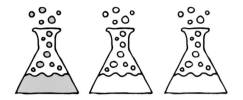

MARSHMALLOW IGLOO

Marshmallows and toothpicks are a winning combo when it comes to STEAM building activities. There are unlimited possibilities in what you can create when given these two simple supplies and asked to build. This activity focuses on building an igloo.

MATERIALS

° 1 bag of jumbo marshmallows
° 1 bag of mini-marshmallows
° 1 box of toothpicks

DIRECTIONS

Build an igloo with about 30 jumbo marshmallows, a couple of handfuls of mini-marshmallows and about 50 toothpicks. You can build the igloo however you want, but if you want a starting point, try to start building the base of the igloo with the big marshmallows and leave a space for the opening of the igloo.

THE HOWS AND WHYS

The toothpicks make perfect connectors for the marshmallows and allow for simple 3-D structures to be built. This activity allows you to take a shape you are familiar with (an igloo) and put your own unique spin on designing and building one.

VARIATION

For a simpler variation, try using a clear, plastic cup turned upside down as a base and glue the marshmallows to the cup to make your igloo.

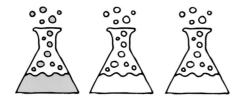

SPRAY PAINT SNOW

Have you ever tried using watercolors to spray paint the snow? This fun process art technique will have you looking at all that snow as a blank canvas waiting to be painted!

MATERIALS

- Spray bottles
- Water
- Liquid food coloring or liquid watercolor paints
- Snow

DIRECTIONS

Once you get the wonderful news that there is freshly fallen snow on the ground, it's time to make your spray bottles. Fill 1 empty spray bottle with water. Add about 10 drops of color (more or less depending on the size of your bottle). Screw the lid on and you are good to go. Make as many colors as possible, but at minimum try to make red, yellow and blue. Bundle up and head outside to get busy painting. Build a snowman and use the spray colors to give him some clothing like a tie-dye shirt or polka dot pants.

THE HOWS AND WHYS

Process art is a technique where the act of making the art is more important than the end result. This activity is very open-ended and encourages creativity by allowing you to paint the snow in any way you wish. The motion of squeezing the spray bottle is also excellent in developing fine motor skills.

VARIATIONS

Don't want to go outside? No problem! Get some snow and put it in a large baking pan and decorate this snow with your spray bottles. Or make mini-snowmen in the baking sheet and decorate your mini-snowmen with the spray bottles. Try using squeeze bottles for even more fun!

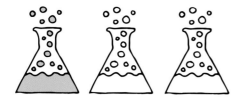

MULTI-COLORED SNOW GLOBES

Here's a fun way to demonstrate how water turns from liquid to solid while bringing some color outside on a snowy day.

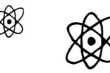

MATERIALS

- Food coloring or liquid watercolors
- Latex balloons (standard size)
- Water

DIRECTIONS

Add about 5 drops of food coloring to the inside of an empty balloon. Then fill the balloon with water until it is a full handful but only about one-quarter full. Tie the balloon and shake it a bit so the color mixes together. Fill more balloons using different colors. Now place the balloons outside. The temperature must be below 32°F (0°C) so that the water in the balloons will freeze. Wait several hours or overnight. Once the balloons are frozen, cut and peel them off and you will see beautiful colored globes! Leave them outside for decoration and they will stay for as long as the temperature stays below freezing. Watch how they melt when the temperature rises.

THE HOWS AND WHYS

When water is in its liquid state, its molecules are constantly moving around and never staying in the same place. When the water freezes, the molecules slow down and stop moving, causing the water to turn to ice.

VARIATION

Bring the frozen globes inside and over the sink or in a baking dish, use droppers to apply warm water and melt the globes. Try adding salt as well to see if it changes how the globes melt.

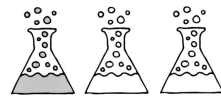

Adult Assistance Required

INSTANT FOG

One of the worst parts of winter if you live in a cold climate is the bitterly cold temperatures that sometimes occur. Here is an activity that makes those days a bit less dreadful and actually a lot of fun!

MATERIALS

- Boiling water (for adult use only)
- Cup

DIRECTIONS

This activity works best when temperatures are in single digits or below 0°F (-18°C). Since this activity deals with boiling hot water, adult participation is required for all steps. Have an adult help you boil the water. Once the water is boiling, the adult should pour the water into a cup, take it outside and throw it into the air. Be sure the area you throw the hot water is clear of any people. What do you see? It appears the hot water turns to fog as it hits the air and evaporates, causing no water to fall to the ground! Amazing!

THE HOWS AND WHYS

What is actually happening here is that the hot water is freezing and morphing from a liquid state to a solid state. The water freezes into very small ice crystals that appear like fog to us. So cool!

VARIATION

Try blowing a bubble outside when the temperature is below 0°F (-18°C). Get the bubble to land without popping by applying a small amount of bubble solution to a plate and landing the bubble on the plate. Watch the ice crystals form as the bubble freezes.

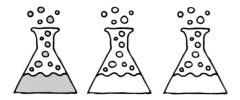

CANDY SNOWFLAKES

Although actual snowflakes are not perfectly symmetrical, they have the general appearance of symmetry. For this fun activity, you will use gumdrops and toothpicks to make candy snowflakes.

MATERIALS

∘ Toothpicks
∘ Gumdrops (Marshmallows, grapes or jellybeans work well too!)

DIRECTIONS

Stick some toothpicks into the gumdrops. Make the shape of a snowflake by connecting gumdrops with toothpicks in them. You make the snowflake symmetrical by making it look identical on both sides.

THE HOWS AND WHYS

Symmetry happens when something is made up of exactly similar parts around an axis or facing each other. It is pleasing to the eye to look at things that have symmetry. Snowflakes look the same on both sides but are actually not exactly symmetrical.

VARIATIONS

Try making the snowflake three dimensional (3-D) instead of two dimensional (2-D). What other symmetrical objects can you make using the same materials?

8

SENSORY
STEAM IDEAS

Sensory play is when one or more of the senses (see, hear, taste, touch or smell) are engaged and emphasized in an activity. Integrating sensory play into an activity is a great way to engage in a deeper way and make an activity that much more fun! The following activities were developed with a focus on engaging one of the senses and are guaranteed to make for an entertaining learning experience.

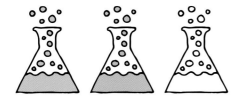

GOOGLY EYES SENSORY BAG

Sensory bags are so simple to set up and can be utilized for a variety of activities! In this activity, you are going to focus on making faces and studying the parts of a face by placing eyes on monsters.

MATERIALS

- 1-gallon (3.8-L) resealable plastic freezer bag
- 1 black permanent marker
- 1 cup (240 ml) hair gel or anti-bacterial hand gel
- 10–15 googly eyes with nonstick backs
- Painter's tape or clear packing tape

DIRECTIONS

Draw some monsters on the outside of the freezer bag with the marker. Don't give the monsters eyes! Add the hair gel or anti-bacterial gel to the freezer bag. (I like using colored hair gel, but clear will work as well, and if you can't find colored, just add a few drops of food coloring to the gel.) Finally, add some googly eyes to the bag. Seal the bag and apply tape to the top and bottom of the bag to secure it to a flat (preferably white or light colored) surface. Move the eyes around the bag to give the monsters different sets of eyes. Since they are monsters, they can have more than two eyes! Where do eyes go on a normal person? How many eyes do people have? How far apart should eyes be? Do the monsters look strange if their eyes are too close together or too far apart?

THE HOWS AND WHYS

All human faces have 2 eyes, a nose and a mouth. We are able to recognize people we know by their faces and how these features are arranged and sized. Each person is unique. Our face contains 3 of the 5 senses: sight, smell and taste (and hearing if you count ears)! This activity is considered sensory because of the touch aspect of the sensory bag. Moving the eyes around through the hair gel makes for a unique touch experience.

VARIATION

A fun facial recognition exercise is to take some photos of famous people or people you know and turn them upside down. Now try to identify the people. You will find it is much more difficult when they are upside down.

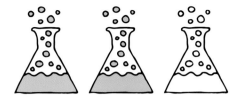

SLIME BUBBLES

Slime is such a fun sensory material as well as a great way to learn about polymers and non-Newtonian fluids. But did you know you can also blow bubbles in slime?

THE HOWS AND WHYS

Slime is ideal for sensory play as its unique properties make it fun to touch, stretch and play with. Slime is both a polymer and a non-Newtonian fluid. Non-Newtonian fluids behave differently than normal fluids such as water. If you blow the bubbles slowly, the slime will expand into a large bubble, but if you blow the bubble too quickly the slime will pop before getting very big as the chemical bonds are broken.

MATERIALS

○ ½ cup (120 ml) white or clear glue
○ ½ tsp baking soda
○ Liquid food coloring
○ 1 bowl
○ 1 spoon
○ 2 tbsp (30 ml) contact lens solution
○ Vegetable oil (optional)
○ 1 straw

DIRECTIONS

Mix together the glue, baking soda and a few drops of food coloring in the bowl using a spoon. When fully mixed and the color is solid, slowly add the contact lens solution. Keep adding a little bit at a time until the mixture stops sticking to the walls of the bowl. Add a few drops of oil if you want to help keep the slime from sticking to your hands. You should now be able to stretch and play with the slime. To make bubbles, lay the slime flat on a table or other flat surface, insert a straw into the slime and blow. Does it work better to blow softer or harder? How big can you make the bubble before it pops?

VARIATION

Once you have mastered blowing a bubble in the slime, try making a double bubble (a bubble within a bubble) or a triple bubble.

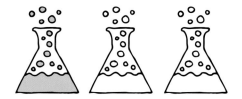

2-INGREDIENT SOAP PUTTY

Putty is another slime-like substance that is fun to play with and has some interesting properties. This simple putty recipe uses only 2 ingredients and will entertain you for hours with its fun sensory squishiness!

MATERIALS

- ½ cup (64 g) cornstarch, plus extra if needed
- ¼ cup (60 ml) clear dish or hand soap, plus extra if needed
- 1 bowl
- 1 spatula

DIRECTIONS

Add the cornstarch and soap to the bowl and mix well with the spatula. If the mixture is still sticky after mixing, add some more cornstarch. If the mixture is dry, add some more soap. Once the mixture starts to behave like putty (where it stretches but doesn't stick to your hands), you will know you have the right balance of ingredients.

THE HOWS AND WHYS

This putty is made with cornstarch, which means it is a non-Newtonian fluid. Non-Newtonian fluids behave quite differently than normal fluids. When a non-Newtonian fluid is pulled apart quickly (applying stress to it), it acts like a solid and the putty breaks apart. But when pressure is applied slowly and the putty is pulled apart slowly, it behaves more like a fluid and the putty stretches into long strings as the bonds are not broken.

VARIATION

Once you are finished playing with your putty, try using it as a bar of soap! Get your hands wet and rub them on the putty. Since the putty is made with soap, you will find some of the soap comes off and coats your hands! Be sure to rinse your hands off the same way you would when washing with regular soap.

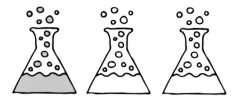

NATURE SENSORY WALK

Getting out in nature is a wonderful sensory activity! From all the sights and smells of nature, to the sounds, textures and even tastes (sometimes) of the objects we find, there is an abundance of opportunities to stimulate all of our senses!

THE HOWS AND WHYS

As you can see from this activity, going on a nature walk is one of the best ways to engage the senses and practice STEAM concepts simply, and with little preparation!

VARIATION

Come up with a mission for your nature walk. Try making DIY binoculars using empty toilet paper rolls glued together and spot interesting things using your binoculars.

MATERIALS

◦ Walking shoes
◦ A basket to collect items

DIRECTIONS

Decide what you will look for on your nature walk and what, if any, items you'll collect along the way. The possibilities are endless but here are some ideas:

•   Look for objects of all different colors and see who can collect the widest variety of colors.

•   Collect items such as leaves, sticks, wildflowers and more to make an art project. When the walk is complete, glue the items on paper to make a beautiful creation.

•   Collect items such as sticks and rocks to build a structure. When the walk is complete, use them to build a structure.

•   Collect unique items you don't see often and see who can find the most interesting object.

•   Count how many birds, rabbits or squirrels you see on your walk.

•   Count how many steps it takes to walk to certain landmarks such as a tree, the stream or a trailhead.

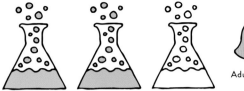

Adult Assistance Required

CALM DOWN BUILDING BLOCK SENSORY BOTTLE

Calm down sensory bottles are great for kids of any age to play with. They are calming to play with when you are feeling anxious and a simple way for young kids to examine small pieces they are too small to play with. You can also examine them and try to understand how they work. Once created, these bottles can be enjoyed for years!

MATERIALS

- Water
- Clear 500-ml water bottle
- ⅔ cup (160 ml) clear glue
- 45–50 small building block pieces, such as LEGOS
- Silver and white glitter (optional)
- Super glue (for adult use only)

DIRECTIONS

Pour the water into the bottle until it is halfway full. Add the glue. At this point, there should still be some space at the top of the bottle. Add the building block pieces. Use a variety of colors. Add some glitter to the mixture if you wish. Fill any remaining space with water so that it's almost filled to the top. Screw the lid on and shake up the bottle. Notice how the toy pieces and glitter move in slow motion through the bottle. Once everything stops moving or slows down, flip the bottle over and watch everything start moving again! If you are satisfied with how the bottle looks, remove the lid and have an adult add some super glue to the rim of the bottle. Replace the cap immediately to permanently seal the lid to the bottle.

THE HOWS AND WHYS

Notice how the toy bricks seem to move in slow motion through the liquid. This is because you added glue to the water, and glue has a higher viscosity than water. Viscosity in liquids determines how fast or slow a liquid is able to flow. The slower a liquid flows, the higher the viscosity.

VARIATIONS

Try using giant water beads or any other small objects you can find around the house. Use a mixture of items that float in water and sink and you will see them pass each other each time the bottle is flipped. Try using other liquids to test their viscosity, such as dish soap, corn syrup or any other liquids you can find around the house.

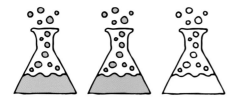

PLAYDOUGH CREATURES

Playdough is such a great medium for creating all kinds of creatures and structures. And when you add items like googly eyes, straws and craft sticks to the mix, the results are amazing!

MATERIALS

- Playdough, 1 or many colors
- Googly eyes
- Straws cut into small pieces
- Craft matchsticks

DIRECTIONS

Set up a play area with all the loose parts laid out and then build playdough creatures using all the parts on the table. That's it! Let the creativity flow and see what you can come up with. Notice how the straws, matchsticks and googly eyes will stick in the playdough. Talk through your design process and develop a story around the creature you are building.

THE HOWS AND WHYS

Open-ended play is so important for building problem-solving skills and creativity. Developing a story around the creature you build allows for further creativity and complexity.

VARIATION

Use the same materials (minus the googly eyes) to build a structure like a house or car instead of a creature.

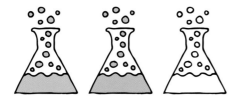

SWIRLING CANDY COLORS (OOBLECK)

Oobleck is one of the coolest fluids on the planet! It behaves very differently than most liquids, and in this activity, you are going to add some candy and make swirling colors with it!

MATERIALS

- 1 cup (128 g) cornstarch
- ½ cup (120 ml) water
- 1 bowl
- 1 spoon or spatula
- Shallow tray
- Skittles or M&M's candies or food coloring

DIRECTIONS

To make the oobleck, add the cornstarch and water to the bowl and mix slowly with the spoon. Once the ingredients are mixed thoroughly with no clumps, your oobleck is complete. If it looks clumpy add some more water. If it looks too liquidy (and you can't pick up a ball of it) then it's too wet, and you need to add some more cornstarch. Pour the oobleck slowly into the tray. Add a few pieces of candy or drops of food coloring if you don't have candy. Slowly tilt the tray so the oobleck moves around and watch the colors start to slowly swirl through the mixture!

THE HOWS AND WHYS

Oobleck is a non-Newtonian fluid. These fluids behave very differently than normal fluids. As you apply pressure to it, it hardens and when you let it sit, it turns back into a liquid.

VARIATION

Make some oobleck just to play with! Try rolling it into a ball and then letting the ball sit in the palm of your hand. You will see the ball turn back into a fluid once you stop rolling it and applying pressure to it. Amazing!

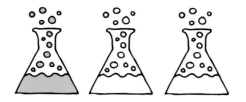

HAND BUBBLES

Bubbles are so fascinating and fun to blow and play with, but did you know you can blow bubbles using only your hand? This fun, sensory activity will allow you to explore how bubbles form and how to blow them using only your hands!

MATERIALS

- 2½ tbsp (38 ml) dish soap
- 1 cup (240 ml) water
- 1 bowl

DIRECTIONS

To make your bubble solution, mix together the dish soap and water in the bowl. Dip the hand you want to blow the bubbles with in the solution so it is covered in bubble mix. Curl your index finger in to make a dime-sized circle and use your thumb to hold the finger in place (almost like making an OK sign). Dip your index finger in the bubble mix, lift it out and blow gently through the hole. If your hand is covered in the solution, a bubble should start forming from the dime-sized circle your index finger formed. And if the rest of your fingers are coated and out of the way as much as possible, they will not cause the bubble to pop. Pinch the hole closed and face your palm up to hold the bubble in your hand. Amazing!

THE HOWS AND WHYS

Since your hand was coated in bubble solution, the bubble didn't pop when touching your fingers or hand. This also allowed you to hold the bubble once it was complete.

VARIATION

Try dipping a finger from your free hand into the bubble solution and then insert that finger into the bubble you've blown. Your finger will pass through to the center of the bubble without popping it!

ACKNOWLEDGMENTS

I'm enormously grateful to all the people who helped make this book possible. First and foremost, I'm so thankful to Page Street Publishing for giving me the opportunity to publish this book. Marissa Giambelluca and Meg Baskis have been so supportive throughout the writing process and a dream to work with. I couldn't have asked for a better experience.

A big thanks to my awesome family and friends! My parents, Joe and Joan, and sister, Lisa, supported and encouraged me throughout this entire journey. I'm also incredibly blessed to have the best husband in the world. Thank you, Tony, for the constant support that came in many forms, from testing activities to encouraging me to follow my dreams! None of this would be possible without your guidance, encouragement and love. And a special thanks to Zanny Oltman, Deena Dolce O'Connor and Rachael Herbert for all your support, guidance and friendship.

A big note of gratitude to Chloe LaFrance for all the beautiful photography that made the book really come to life.

And most importantly, thank you to my boys Nate, Dylan, Oliver and Alexander who are the inspiration and motivation for everything I do. The curiosity and joy I see in your eyes is the reason this book exists.

And lastly, thank you to all Raising Dragons supporters, whose constant encouragement has allowed me to continue my creative mission to keep kids learning and having fun!

ABOUT THE AUTHOR

Andrea Scalzo Yi is the founder and creative force behind Raising Dragons, a company with a mission to inspire parents and educators with simple ways to play and educate kids. A wife and mother of four energetic sons, her background in both engineering and fashion gave her a passion for STEAM activities and led her to create Raising Dragons (www.raisingdragons.com) where she shares simple educational activities that allow parents and educators to make learning fun. Featured in articles by *Good Housekeeping*, Hearst Digital Media and Brit+Co, Raising Dragons has amassed more than 850,000 followers across platforms including Facebook, Instagram, Pinterest and YouTube, and its videos have been viewed more than 100 million times.

INDEX